INSIDE THE DMZ

CHRISTOPHER WASHINGTON

ISBN: 978-1-7334447-0-5 (paperback)
ISBN: 978-1-7334447-1-2 (e-book)
ISBN: 978-1-7334447-2-9 (hardback)

Library of Congress Control Number: 2019912364

Copyediting by Author One Stop, Inc. (www.AuthorOneStop.com)

Design and production by Joanne Shwed, Backspace Ink (www.backspaceink.com)

All my love to my grandchildren
Casey and Courtney

ACKNOWLEDGMENTS

*To Tim Hallinan, renowned author and writing instructor:
Thanks for believing in me and recognizing that I had a book inside me.*

*To my writing group participants Linda Hobrock, Susi Rajah and
Catherine Saykaly-Stevens: Thank you for allowing me to be part of
your group and for your encouragement. Our group's requirement
that each person write something and bring it to our weekly
meetings kept the creative process going and allowed for constructive
feedback and invaluable recommendations from everyone.*

*To my family and friends: Thank you for your support and, in
particular, my daughter Nicole for her computer skills and patience
without which this book could never have been written.*

*Finally, thanks to my editors Randy Peyser (Author One
Stop) and Joanne Shwed (Backspace Ink): Thank you
for your help and professionalism in guiding me through
the process of bringing this book to completion.*

CONTENTS

AUTHOR'S NOTE

THIS IS NONFICTION. The events, conversations and experiences detailed herein are true and have been faithfully rendered as I remembered them to the best of my ability. Some names, identities and circumstances have been changed in order to protect the integrity and anonymity of the various individuals involved.

Though conversations come from memory, they are not written word-for-word documentation. Rather, I've retold them in a way that evokes the real feeling and meaning of what was said and in keeping with the true essence of the mood and spirit of the traumatic events affecting the lives of these brave men serving duty inside the DMZ.

LIST OF ACRONYMS

D/O	duty officer
DMZ	[Korean] Demilitarized Zone
GI	army soldier
JSA	Joint Security Area
KATUSA	Korean Augmentation to the United States Army
KP	kitchen police
MP	Military Police
NCO	Noncommissioned Officers [Club]
OCS	Officer Candidate School
PX	post exchange
ROK	Republic of Korea
UCLA	University of California at Los Angeles
UN	United Nations
UNC	United Nations Command [forces]
USO	United Service Organizations
VD	venereal disease

"STOP: Southern Boundary of Demilitarized Zone"

PROLOGUE

THE YEAR IS 1964, and Korea is still at war. A peace treaty has never been signed. The forces of the United Nations (UN) and the Republic of South Korea on one side and the army of North Korea on the other are not actively engaged in combat, but they still oppose each other every day along a 151-mile strip that bisects the country of Korea. This situation has existed since a truce was signed on July 27, 1953.

The Korean Demilitarized Zone (DMZ) is the 4,000-meter (2.5-mile) wide buffer zone that runs across the Korean Peninsula from the Han River estuary in the west to just below the 39th parallel on the east coast.

Down the center of this buffer zone, which has grown thick with underbrush in the years since the truce was signed, is the Military Demarcation Line, which is marked by 1,292 intermittently spaced signs. Each sign is printed in Korean and English on the side facing south and Korean and Chinese on the side facing north. This is the line where ground contact between the opposing forces ended at the moment of ceasefire in 1953 and now separates the Republic of Korea (ROK) in the south from the communist north.[1]

---

1. United Nations Command/Military Armistice Commission booklet, *The Longest Armistice.*

The Joint Security Area (JSA), located in the city of Panmunjom and within the DMZ, is the neutral ground on which negotiations between the North Korean communists and the United Nations Command (UNC) are carried out. Security in the conference area is provided jointly by Military Police (MP) from both sides. Each side is permitted to have a maximum of 35 security personnel on duty in the conference area of the JSA at one time. It is perhaps the only U.S. military group in the world that performs duty jointly with its enemy.

The most frustrating, nerve-straining duty in Korea is that served by the officers and enlisted men assigned to the US Army Support Group in the JSA. Although not a tactical military unit, these men are located in a unique spot as their motto suggests—"IN FRONT OF THEM ALL"—in front of the approximately 37,000 US troops that are stationed below them in South Korea. Also, they stand in the very vulnerable position of being squarely in the path of an invasion of the south by the North Koreans, which could come at any time. These men are isolated by the Imjin River, which separates the JSA from South Korea, and by the DMZ on the northern side. They are isolated more profoundly by having the responsibility of working in an area where one wrong move or one loss of self-control on the part of any person, whether a private or a general, could sever the truce and start both sides shooting at each other once again.

I, CHRISTOPHER WASHINGTON, a 23-year-old black American, was assigned to the JSA in January 1964 after completing 16 weeks of basic and MP training. However, my journey to this spot began when, in early August 1963, I received a notice from my draft board in Los Angeles with greetings and an invitation to report on August 22, 1963, for induction into the US Army for 24 months.

I had foolishly let my college courses drop below 12 units, which was considered full-time status and would have kept me out of the draft. I did not think the Selective Service board checked on things like that, but they did. So, being drafted wasn't a surprise, but being put on an airplane and flown to Fort Leonard Wood, Missouri, for basic training was. I had assumed that I would do basic training at Fort Ord, California, like most other inductees from my community. Because of the ever-escalating Vietnam War, I later learned about the buildup of US military forces and that Fort Ord could not handle any more trainees.

I WAS RAISED in San Antonio, Texas, and attended segregated schools until my family moved to Los Angeles, California, in 1955 when I was 15 years old—before I could experience any serious incidents of racism in the American South. Sure, we blacks attended segregated schools, drank out of water fountains that said "COLORED" and had to sit in the back of the bus. I was born into those incidents of discrimination, so I was not acutely aware of racism per se. However, the blatant acts of discrimination and bigotry I experienced while in uniform in southern cities around Fort Leonard Wood in Missouri and Fort Gordon in Augusta, Georgia, would later cause me to seriously question myself and my commitment to die for my country.

ON AUGUST 28, 1963—six days after I was drafted—more than 250,000 people gathered in the nation's capital for the March on Washington and to hear Martin Luther King, Jr.'s historic "I Have a Dream" speech, which called for racial equality. Less than three weeks later, a bomb exploded in the 16th Street Baptist Church in Birmingham, Alabama, killing four young black girls. Earlier in the year, blacks had participated in sit-ins and Freedom Rides on buses in an effort to desegregate the South. Then, exactly three months from the day I was drafted—November 22, 1963—President John F. Kennedy was assassinated in Dallas, Texas.

This was the climate in the United States as I began my 24-month commitment to serve in the military. Also, it was a time when some young American men were fleeing to Canada or hastily getting married in an effort to avoid the draft.

I WAS ASSIGNED to the JSA as an MP and worked in that capacity for about a month before being reassigned as my company's finance clerk.

Having worked as an MP and performing guard duty in the DMZ, I experienced the sheer terror and vulnerability one feels while working daily in an atmosphere that could at any minute cost you your life. As the company finance clerk, I also served in the unique capacity where I came into contact with all of the approximately 145 military personnel assigned to the Support Group.

My position allowed me to witness in many respects how these men adapted (or didn't adapt) to working and living in such a hazardous environment. Like them, I found duty in the JSA to be lonely and, over weeks and months, saw how it gradually changed a man. I will never forget my one-year assignment in the JSA. It was a year filled with laughter and tragedy, assaults, a suicide, land-mine injuries, prisoner exchanges, a court-martial and, yes, infidelity.

IN THE BEGINNING

I HAVE NEVER heard of Fort Leonard Wood, Missouri, or of the major general for whom the fort is named. It is August 22, 1963, and I am beginning basic training in the army. In an 1886 campaign against the Apache Indian Chief Geronimo, General Leonard Wood won a Medal of Honor for heroic actions in this place. Also, he was considered a leading Republican presidential contender but lost the nomination to Warren G. Harding in 1920, who was subsequently elected and served as our 29th president from 1921 until his death in office in 1923.

Located southwest of St. Louis, this 71,000-acre fort lies within the Mark Twain National Forest in the Missouri Ozarks. The small town of Waynesville sits about a mile outside the main gate. Summer in Missouri is a brutal time to go through basic training, particularly when almost all physical activities are conducted outside in extremely high temperatures and humid conditions. There is a rumor that a famous radio gossip reporter lost a son here a few years ago while going through basic training in the heat.

The reporter later would comment on the air, "Pray for your son if he's sent to Fort Leonard Wood, Missouri."

The fort is called "Little Korea," presumably by vets who liken the physical environment to that country.

In any event, I survive two months of training. I try out for and make the post football team. The team is undefeated, and their next game is against a navy team at their base in Tennessee. I play three games before shipping off to my second eight weeks of training in Augusta, Georgia. I wish I could play with the team the whole season to see if our winning streak continues.

Other than my desire to stay and play football, I am ready to leave. The area surrounding Fort Leonard Wood is not open to minorities. We are warned not to even try to go into nightclubs and restaurants in Waynesville. The larger city of Springfield is about 100 miles away, but racism is blatant there too.

Fort Leonard Wood

MY SECOND EIGHT weeks of training is at MP school at Fort Gordon, Georgia. It is late October and the civil rights movement is beginning to gain momentum. However, the movement is being met by hateful, ugly clashes among nonviolent protesters, southern officials and policemen. Daily television reports show Birmingham Police Chief Bull Connor and members of the Ku Klux Klan ("Klansmen") attacking

18

nonviolent protesters with clubs, water hoses and dogs. Man, the Deep South is a place I don't want to be in right now. Even more frightening, I could spend my whole two years of enlistment in one of these southern hellholes.

The MP school at Fort Gordon consists of several classrooms and a makeshift city block for tactical training—a fake city like one might find on a Hollywood studio lot. Also, it has a bleacher area where outside lectures are conducted.

IT IS NOVEMBER 22, 1963. In the morning, we participate in an exercise at the makeshift city where civilian or enemy cardboard figures pop up from around corners or in a window, and we make a split-second decision whether or not to shoot them. It is fun but, needless to say, we shoot a lot of innocent civilians.

At about 2 p.m., my class returns from lunch. We settle on the hard seats for another couple of hours of a lecture on crowd control. It is a cold but shiny day; the warm sunlight feels good on my face. Unlike at Fort Leonard Wood, I am glad to be outside in the fresh air.

At the lectern is Sergeant Jennings, explaining what we did wrong earlier and how to correct it. As he begins to speak, I notice a jeep pulling up several feet from the field. A captain gets out and approaches the bleachers. As he climbs the steps to the lectern, he apologizes to Sergeant Jennings for the interruption but says that he has an important announcement.

"President John Kennedy has just been shot by an unknown assassin in Dallas, Texas. Thus far, we do not know if the shooting of the president is part of a further pending attack on the United States. Therefore, the United States military has been put on alert. All classes are suspended, and you are to immediately report back to your company for further instructions."

The class is stunned, not believing what we have just heard.

As we pile out of the bleachers and head across the field, there is an air of jubilation among some of the southern army soldiers (GIs) in the class. They are actually happy about the president being killed. These southern rednecks apparently didn't like Kennedy's support of the civil rights movement and the changes that were rapidly coming about in the country.

A sickening feeling comes over me, knowing that I will have to live and work with these guys for another few months. It's one thing to face discrimination from townspeople, but it's another to know that some of the same types of people are living in the barracks with you, and some day you may have to rely on them in battle.

"How can I ever trust them?" I wonder. "Can they trust me? Am I willing to give up my life for them?"

I guess I will never know until the opportunity presents itself. This is the last day of MP school, and I am elated. I don't care where my next assignment is as long as it is out of the American South.

IT IS EARLY MORNING, December 18, 1963. Our new assignments are posted on the bulletin board outside the recreation room. My friend John Gibson and I rush over and crowd around the board with our fellow trainees, desperately searching for our names. John has been with me in basic training at Fort Leonard Wood, and we have both been assigned the military occupation status of MP. He is also a black American, a native of Detroit, Michigan, and about the same 6-foot height as I am. He has recently married and is deeply in love with his wife. He is hoping that his new assignment will be at a place where his wife can join him.

We make our way close to the bulletin board, and my heart sinks as I go down the list of names. All I can see are assignments to companies in Vietnam. Finally, I find my name and, to my surprise, it says something different: "Joint Security Area, Panmunjom, Korea." John finds his name and his assignment is the same. Again, we are going to the same place! I am thrilled to be getting out of the South, but I can see the disappointment in John's face. He knows that Korea is called an "isolated tour of duty," which means that no families can come along.

"I'm sorry, John," I say as we walk toward the mess hall. "I know you were hoping to stay in the States, but it could have been worse. Did you see all those guys going to Vietnam?"

"Yeah, I guess we lucked out," he says, but I can still sense his disappointment.

MY TRAVELING ORDERS say that I am to report to the Oakland, California, Debarkation Center on January 4, 1964, for subsequent deployment to Korea. This is great news since it allows me to travel to the west coast and spend two weeks at home with my family and girlfriend Evelyn during the Christmas holidays.

Eve and I have been going together for almost five years and have talked about marriage, but we put it off because we were both busy working and trying to get our college education, although she is doing a better job of it than I am. She will be finishing at the University of California at Los Angeles (UCLA) within a year. She moved to Los Angeles several years ago to go to college. We met at a party in 1959 and have mostly been together ever since.

By getting married, I could avoid the military draft. However, to me, that would be cowardly, not to mention marrying for the wrong reason. My three older brothers have all served honorably in various branches of the military, and I will be no exception. They are great role models, and I look up to each one of them.

On January 3, 1964—the day before I am supposed to leave—Eve and I decide to get married anyway. We marry at the municipal courthouse in downtown Los Angeles by Judge Nora Gannon, a colorful judge who wears big, beautiful hats during her ceremonies. My brother Ernest serves as my best man, and my sister Carol is the maid of honor. Eve has no family in California, but her mother, who lives in Chicago, has given us her blessings long distance and wishes us the best of happiness.

THE NEXT DAY is one of the saddest of my life. I have to leave my new bride less than 24 hours after being married. I do not realize the emotional impact this would have on me until it is time to kiss her and say goodbye again at the Los Angeles International Airport right before I am to board a PSA flight to Oakland.

The last time I left in August, we assumed that I would be going to Fort Ord and have the opportunity to come home within a few weeks, so our parting was not as emotional. However, it didn't work out that way with me being sent to Fort Leonard Wood, so we ended up being apart for four months. This time it will be even longer—another year.

"After I finish school, I'll find a better job and have a nice setup for us when you come back," Eve says. "I hope you can be reassigned someplace nearby for your final eight months."

"That's too far ahead for me to think about. Anyway, right now, I don't want to stop hugging and kissing you."

"Know that I love you and will be waiting for you. Please promise me that you won't let anything happen to you over in Korea. And you'd better write, or I'll be angry. God, I pray that you will not end up in Vietnam." She hugs me tightly, burying her face in my uniform.

"Ah, don't worry about that. I'm an MP, and all we do is direct traffic anyway. We don't get involved in combat. I promise to write as often as I can. I love you, Mrs. Washington."

We kiss for the last time, and I force myself to pull away from her to board the plane. I realize the agony that John is going through back at Fort Gordon, Georgia.

WELCOME TO KOREA.
NOW GO HOME

AFTER I STAY at the Oakland Debarkation Center for three days, my name is finally called for a flight to Japan and then on to Korea. During these three days, there is nothing to do but wait until the next morning to see if my name is called for debarkation. I try to call Eve every day, but the eight telephone booths outside our barracks are constantly occupied by other guys who are trying to get in one last conversation with a wife or sweetheart. There must be about 2,000 GIs waiting to be deployed, and most are going to Vietnam.

I run into my friend James Tyler from basic training at Fort Leonard Wood. He is being assigned to a base in Japan. We exchange addresses and promise to stay in touch. The person I do not see in Oakland is John Gibson. I wonder what happened to him.

I LEAVE THE STATES on January 7, 1964, flying military air transportation after a short bus ride from Oakland up to Travis Air Force Base in northern California. The Air Force airplane has no windows except for a couple of round glass portals on each side. It is just as well since all I can see for the 15-hour flight to Tokyo is the Pacific Ocean. The seats on the plane are benches, facing each other on each side of the plane, which is typically seen in a movie where paratroopers sit and stare at each other as they wait to jump.

We have no stewardesses but rather Airmen who serve us box lunches. However, I am glad to be traveling by air rather than by ship after hearing the many horror stories of those who have made the two-week trip by sea, which is the customary travel mode for military personnel assigned to the Far East. Seasickness is a common trait among the travelers, and one also has to work during those two weeks including kitchen police (KP) and guard duty.

While in Japan for a few days, we are housed at the Kishine Barracks in the city of Yokohama where, at the end of World War II and the defeat of Japan, military personnel rested and relaxed. Ironically, I can hear Japanese soldiers doing calisthenics at 4:30 a.m. at their military installation next door while we sleep until 6:00 a.m.

"They will probably catch us sleeping again one day when we should be awake," I think.

ON JANUARY 13, I board a flight for the approximately two-hour trip to Korea. I arrive at the Replacement Detachment Center at Kimpo International Airport, Pusan, South Korea, and a driver is dispatched from the JSA to get me.

It is shortly after 1:00 p.m. when Sergeant Edward Johnson comes into the Replacement Detachment Center and signs me out for reassignment to the JSA. We go outside, and I throw my duffel bag in the rear of his open-top jeep. It is cold, extremely cold. Heavy snow is pushed aside to make a path for the road. I hope we don't have too far to travel in this open jeep.

"Where you from, Washington?" Johnson asks.

"LA. Los Angeles."

He laughs. "Well, I guess this is not your kind of weather."

"Not hardly. Although doing training at MP school in Georgia the last few months sort of prepared me for this. It is cold there too."

"Yeah, I trained there myself a few years ago."

"So, you're an MP too?" I ask.

"Yes. Almost everyone in the JSA is an MP. Do you know anything about where you're being assigned?"

"No. My knowledge of Korea and its history is limited. I'm just happy that I didn't have to go to Vietnam like 90% of the guys in my training class."

"Well, where you're being assigned up by the DMZ is no piece of cake either."

Johnson explains that the JSA is located within the DMZ, which is neutral ground where negotiations between the North Korean communists and the UNC are carried out. Security in the conference area is provided jointly by MPs from both sides.

"There are no communications with the North Koreans except by our representatives at the truce table. We guard our buildings, and they guard theirs. We kind of silently coexist. You probably don't know it, but you were hand-picked for assignment to the JSA."

"You're kidding! Now that I think about it, maybe that's why they forced me against my will to go to Leadership School at Fort Gordon for two weeks. My stay in the Deep South was not a pleasant one, so I didn't want to stay down there any longer than I had to."

Johnson is Caucasian, and I am not sure he knows what I am talking about.

"Yeah. When I was there, I remember some of the black soldiers complaining about the way they were treated in town."

"I was in uniform one weekend," I recall, "walking downtown and window shopping, and this merchant comes running out and telling me, 'Boy, if you're not going to come in and buy anything, then get the hell out from in front of my store.' He shook me up so bad that I immediately went back to the fort and never went into town again."

"I'm sorry to hear that," Johnson sympathizes.

After a while, I notice the countryside as we speed along the bumpy, frozen road. All I can see for miles is what appears to be rice paddy fields on each side.

I wonder silently, "What is America's interest in this country? Is it worth fighting a war over? Better still, why do I have to spend a year of my life here? As far as I know, America is not a big rice-eating country."

Sergeant Johnson breaks the silence. "We're going to be coming upon the city of Seoul shortly, and then you will get a chance to see something other than rice paddies."

"Great," I say as my teeth began to chatter from the cold air sweeping across my face.

AS WE APPROACH SEOUL, traffic suddenly comes to a crawl behind a potpourri of Korean and military vehicles and street vendors in carts. Pedestrians weave in and out of traffic, apparently ambivalent to their own safety. The sidewalks are busy with people coming and going. The city reminds me of Chinatown in Los Angeles or San Francisco but on a much bigger scale. I am too cold to notice much of anything else. I only want the traffic to move ahead so we can get to our final destination.

We make our way through Seoul and back onto the highway and head up to the DMZ. Along the way, we pass through several small villages, one of which is the town of Yong Ju Gol.

"Some of our guys come to visit the bars and nightclubs in this village. Also, there's a military base up ahead called Camp Casey—a few miles south and right outside Yong Ju Gol. This is the closet PX [post exchange] where you can buy stuff like candy, cigarettes and toiletries. There's a restaurant where you can buy American food like hamburgers and fries, and they have a movie theater on base that shows the latest American films. I'm sure you'll be spending some of your free time here."

"How do we get here?"

"Military buses travel every hour on the hour from the JSA all the way to Seoul and back, carrying soldiers and civilians who work at the various military installations along the way."

After about 45 minutes, we arrive at a one-lane, narrow truss bridge that spans the Imjin River.

"This is it. This is Freedom Bridge. This river represents roughly the dividing line between South and North Korea—the 38th parallel of latitude that splits the two Koreas. Once we reach the other side, we're at the DMZ, which is a 5-mile-long strip of land up to the North

Korean border. This is where you will live and work for the next 12 months."

Directly across from the U.S. Army base in South Korea known as Camp Casey is a warren of tiny streets lined with nightclubs. Some of the foreign women who were recruited to work at the clubs were horrified when they realized they were expected to prostitute themselves.

Los Angeles Times: Camp Casey

ONCE WE REACH the other side of the bridge, an MP lets us through by raising a black-and-white crossing gate arm, similar to what one would find at a railroad crossing. Then, about 100 yards to the left, we approach the entryway of the JSA and see an overhead sign that reads, "Stop. You're About to Enter the Demilitarized Zone." In addition, there are two 6-foot white signs on each side on the road. One sign is in English and the other is in Korean, and both sides issue warnings about the dangers and prohibitions when proceeding into the DMZ.

My first day is spent with a few other new arrivals, going through an orientation session about the purpose, conduct and responsibilities of personnel serving duty in the JSA. Also, the session covers our treatment and responsibilities to the Korean civilians who are working within our camp area.

Freedom Bridge

The sergeant conducting the session says, "Everybody has a houseboy assigned to them to do things like make up bunks, do laundry, press uniforms, shine boots and polish belt buckles. The houseboy's fees are deducted directly from your pay, so there is never a dispute about their money. And, damn it, don't lay a hand on them! You can be court-martialed for assault. If for some reason you and your houseboy don't get along, go to his supervisor and ask for a replacement," he added emphatically.

On the second day, we take a trip down to I Corps at Camp Casey to be fitted for clothing, which is needed for the extremely cold winter climate. The cotton fatigues, which we normally worked in back in the States, are replaced by a gabardine uniform called "olive greens." Other clothing includes a well-insulated parka with an attached fur-lined hood, a fur-lined cap with flaps that can be pulled down over the ears and scarves to protect the neck area. Also, cloth name tags are made up with our last names.

"Have your houseboys sew on the name tags. They'll also sew on your stripes as you're promoted or demoted, whichever the case may be," the supply clerk advises sarcastically.

Later in the day after returning from Camp Casey, those of us who are working as MPs are taken to the Arms Room for assignment of our .45-caliber weapons and MP arm bands. It is now time to go to work. I am told that I will start this night on the midnight shift.

At first glance, the narrow and somewhat small bridge—known as the Bridge of No Return, which spans the dry, shallow riverbed dividing the north from the south—appears to be necessary but insignificant and unimportant. The floor of the bridge is wooden with a 3-foot-wide wooden railing on each side. Its length is roughly 150 feet. The bridge doesn't have the stature of the Golden Gate Bridge in San Francisco or even the majestic beauty of the tall, scenic Bixby Creek Bridge that spans the deep, mountainous gorges of Monterey, California. This bridge is functional and sturdy. It gets you from one side to the other efficiently but without fanfare except for the rumbling of the wooden floor from vehicles speeding across it.

There is no beauty in this bridge or its drab surrounding area. The road on either side is unpaved dirt. There is a yellow wooden sign at the base that reads "Military Demarcation Line" and "Marker Number 0900."

In September 1953, the agonizing end of the Korean War came right here. Over 12,000 captured and sick UN forces returned home to the south across this bridge, and over 75,000 communist prisoners were returned to the north. In the spring, the riverbed flows from melting snow and in the summer from seasonal rain. Also, according to local legend, in ages past it has run red with blood.

Military checkpoints sit on opposite sides of the bridge, with UNC military personnel on the south side and the Korean People's Army on the north. Walk across, run across or drive across this bridge from the south to the north and you are history. If you're not immediately shot and killed by the North Koreans, then you may be taken prisoner, never to be heard from again. There is no returning if you venture to the wrong side of this bridge.

Bridge of No Return

MY FIRST ASSIGNMENT as an MP in the DMZ is at this checkpoint at the south side of the bridge. It is called the "Loneliest Outpost in the World." I am assigned the midnight shift (12:00 p.m. to 8:30 a.m.). All guard posts are jointly manned by a US MP and an ROK soldier, who is called a KATUSA (Korean Augmentation to the United States Army). The kid assigned with me on this night appears to be no more than 16 years old and scared shitless. That makes two of us. He speaks no

English, but that is not unusual. None of them do, but this is not from lack of trying. All KATUSA soldiers seem to carry a Korean/English dictionary, and most of the time their heads are buried in it while trying to learn the English language. I wonder if they are under some kind of time constraint to learn English for an exam.

Bridge of No Return

The guard shack is approximately 5 feet by 6 feet with a potbelly stove in the middle. There is an unlit lantern hanging in one corner. During our briefing, we are advised not to light it unless absolutely necessary. Our job is to observe the surrounding area, and you can't see outside from a lit structure inside. Some light is provided by the flickering fire through the cracks around the door of the potbelly stove.

It is a cold January night, probably 30 degrees F. A thin sheet of snow is gently falling on the shrubbery. I stare out the window of the guard shack and quietly marvel at the serenity and peacefulness. Coming from California, I have never experienced actual winter seasons.

Snowflakes permeate the cold night air as they fall from the sky. It is beautiful. Then, looking a little bit harder, I can see the cold stare of that damn bridge through the veil of the falling snow, and that's when I snap back into reality—back to the realization of the absolute terror that awaits 150 feet away. All I have are a walkie-talkie, a .45-caliber handgun and a Korean kid who doesn't speak English.

I pace the small enclosure, too nervous to sit down. No one is going to sneak up on me if I can help it. The kid positions his chair in front of the stove, so he can study his book from the light of the fire. At one point, he pokes me on the leg and points at a word in his book. I assume he wants pronunciation.

"Hello," I say, staring at the word.

He tries to say it, but it comes out "ello" or "yellow." (Koreans seemed to have trouble using words that began with "h.")

"Hello," I say again with some irritation in my voice. I am in no mood to be giving English lessons.

AFTER A FEW HOURS, I notice vehicle lights coming down the road from the south. As the lights get closer, I see that it is a US military jeep. The vehicle pulls up to the side of the shack. It is Sergeant Johnson, making his rounds with oil for the stove. I'm sure he is also checking to see that no one is asleep.

"How's your first night going, Chris?" he asks as he pours oil into the stove.

"Fine. No problems."

"You'll get used to it. Duty up here is pretty much uneventful. Like I told you in your briefing, if we don't bother the North Koreans, they won't bother us. They're just as afraid of us as we are of them."

I am very relieved to see another American, and I don't want him to leave. I try to think of something to say to engage him in conversation so he will stay a while longer, but nothing comes out. I don't want fear to show in my voice. Somewhere in my basic training, I remember someone saying that men fight not for God or country and not out of fear of being killed, but because they don't want to show fear. Men do not want to shame themselves by displaying cowardice to their buddies.

"Okay, then. I'll send some relief for you guys in a couple of hours, so you can get some lunch and coffee. See you later, Chris."

"Okay, Sarg."

IN MY 20-SOMETHING YEARS, I have never faced fear before—well, not like this anyway. This is about the fear of dying. Sure, there are moments on the football field when I faced fear of injury or fear of failure. That fear only lasted a few hours. In a game, I am with friends and teammates, facing the enemy together. We huddle up and encourage each other after every play. Here, this is isolation. I am alone. Here, my teammates are several hundred feet up the road in other guard posts or back at the compound. This is a test of courage. During the next 12 months, I am going to spend many more nights here.

"Will I have the mental toughness to stick it out?" I ask myself. "Others have done it, and so will I."

As the great South African leader Nelson Mandela once said, "Courage [is] not the absence of fear, but triumph over it."

AT ABOUT 4:00 A.M., two MPs arrive in an open jeep to relieve us for lunch. The two Caucasian soldiers quickly come into the guard shack after shaking off the snow from their coats.

"Get your ass out of the way," one of the MPs tells the Korean kid as they both shove their way past him, taking off their gloves and rubbing their hands over the potbelly stove.

I'm sure the kid doesn't understand what is said to him, but he still receives the message. He gets up from his chair and goes outside. The small enclosure is not meant for four people, particularly when three are over 6 feet tall.

The arrogant treatment of the kid by the two GIs is my first exposure to the disdain for the Korean people displayed by some Americans. This boy and generations of Koreans to follow are the ones who we are supposedly here to protect.

Surely, the Korean must ask himself, "Who is the real oppressor in our country? Whom should I fear the most?"

I don't like it, but I do not want to get into a confrontation with these two rednecks in the middle of nowhere.

"You chased my partner out," I say jokingly to Bruce Anderson, a Specialist 4 (the next grade above private first class). The other MP is Private First Class James Gray, who has been in Korea for about five months.

"Ah, I was just having a little fun with the kid," says Anderson. "After you've been here for 11 months like I have, you'll see that these KATUSAs aren't worth a shit. You ever drive a jeep?"

"No, but I know how to drive a stick shift. I'll manage," I say.

"Okay. You guys take the jeep and go back to camp for lunch and, goddamn it, don't be all day! We've got to relieve two other checkpoints before the night is through."

I am beginning to dislike Anderson more and more by the minute. I silently hope that I don't turn into an asshole like him after 11 months here.

"Got it. We'll be back as fast as we can."

THE DRIVE BACK to our compound down the slick, dark road is scary since the only light is from the headlights of the jeep. The falling snow makes visibility in front of the jeep no more than 5 or 6 feet. The thick brush on either side of the narrow, two-lane road is close enough to touch. Although this is our section of the DMZ, North Korean infiltrators or spies have been known to come into the area but have never attacked any members of the UNC. Still, the thought is in my mind that it could easily happen.

The speed limit, which is periodically posted alongside the road, is 25 miles per hour, so the drive back to camp seems to take forever. Finally, I can see the lights of the front gate coming into view, which means that we are coming back to the friendly sanctuary of our compound if for no more than 30 precious minutes.

The kid and I make it back to our outpost in about 40 minutes, and the two MPs are on their way to another post. We pull up our chairs around the stove and stick out our hands for warmth. After eating, our eyelids begin to get heavy, and we both start to nod.

AT JUST ABOUT the time I fall asleep, I am awakened by a blaring noise coming from giant loudspeakers on the North Korean side—as if they know our routine of getting sleepy right after lunch. First comes a steady diet of hideous North Korean music for about a half hour. Then I hear a tirade of propaganda in broken English about imperialist Americans occupying their country.

"Hey, sleepy GI. You at the bridge. Welcome to our country."

It takes me a few minutes to realize that the voice is talking to me.

"Shit," I think, "they're talking to me! Can they see inside this dark shack? Are they hiding in the bushes? How do they know I'm a new MP?"

"Why you sit here on our border?" the female voice asks. "We not sitting on coast of California. You should be home right now back in States in bed with black American girlfriend. Tell your captain you want to go home."

She continues her harassment in Korean, presumably directing a similar message to my young Korean friend. He appears to be scared to death. We both stand up and look outside.

The thought of the North Koreans talking to me personally becomes unnerving. This is when I first realize that, in wearing a US military uniform, to the North Koreans I am America, I am the enemy and, at this moment, I am the American imperialist occupying their border.

"Why am I here?" I wonder.

Sadly, I don't have an answer except for the fact that my country drafted me into its army.

Sergeant Johnson had not mentioned this barrage of propaganda in our briefing. I guess he wanted me to experience it firsthand without warning. It certainly got my attention and got me on my feet. I don't close my eyes again for the rest of the morning, knowing that I am being watched.

AT ABOUT 6:00 A.M., I hear the rumbling of the wooden floor of the bridge, indicating a vehicle coming from the north. I quickly move to the door, preparing for the worst. However, the truck, which is loaded with North Koreans guards, slows down briefly as it passes, as if to intimidate us, and then keeps going up to the conference area. Thirty minutes later, the truck comes back, going north across the bridge, presumably with guards going off duty.

Similarly, our canvas-back truck comes back around 8:35 a.m. with replacements. An MP and a KATUSA soldier get out and relieve us from our post.

"How was your night?" the MP asks as we stand outside the shack. "Anything unusual that we should know about?"

"No," I say, "except that some North Korean female talked to us over the loudspeaker for half the night."

The MP laughs. "They know you're new. They are just trying to rattle you. Write up an incident report when you get back to camp. Our command will lodge a complaint at the next truce talks with the North Koreans because there is not supposed to be any harassment of either side's personnel in the DMZ. However, we've complained before about them violating the peace agreement to no avail. They just deny the accusation."

We get into the back of the truck and continue to the other eight checkpoints, exchanging guards. Arriving back in camp, we clear our weapons of ammunition outside the Arms Room and turn them in to the soldier on duty behind the counter. After a quick breakfast in the mess hall, I am off to my bunk to sleep.

I have survived my first night of guard duty at the North Korean border of the DMZ.

CHANGE OF DUTY/ LAND-MINE INCIDENT

THERE ARE NINE different American guard posts in the JSA. Post #4 is located at the base of the Bridge of No Return, and my first two weeks on guard duty are spent at this post. Post #3 is located around the conference buildings. Guards assigned to this post are responsible for providing security to the Switzerland/Sweden (Swiss/ Swede) delegation, which lives and works from their camp just outside the JSA. They are part of the Neutral Nations Supervisory Commission whose mission is to ensure that both sides adhere to the provisions of the Armistice Agreement. The Swiss/Swede delegation represents the UN, and the Czechoslovakia/Poland delegation, whose camp is in North Korea, represents the Korean People's Army.

The security we provide mainly consists of checking the storehouses to the rear of their camp to keep thieves from looting their provisions. Korean thieves foolish enough to venture into the very dangerous DMZ have been known to come from north and south villages close by.

IT'S EARLY FEBRUARY 1964, and I'm into my third week on the midnight shift at Post #3. I am glad to be away from the bridge and the nightly harassment from the North Koreans, although this post is no piece of cake either. About once every hour, we patrol the perimeter of the Swiss/Swede camp to check their buildings. The Swiss/Swede camp is not well lit, so much of the trip around the premises is in the dark, which make us susceptible to surprise attack from thieves if we happen to catch them in the act of looting.

I am assigned to work with the same Korean kid I had the previous week. I guess the army thinks that, by working with the same ROK soldier, some type of bond will form between us. On the first time around the camp, the kid is constantly up my back, almost holding my shirt. He is scared to death. I ignore him, but I reach around and push his arm off me without taking my eyes off the dark path ahead.

Suddenly, we hear a noise in the woods, and the boy is up my back again.

"That was probably an animal. But, goddamn it, your ass is going to get shot if you don't stop jumping on my back!"

I turn and point at him, gesturing to my holstered gun. He gets the message and stays off my back for the rest of the night.

A FEW DAYS LATER, going off duty, Sergeant Johnson tells me that First Sergeant Miller wants to see me after I have breakfast. I cannot imagine what he wants since I have only been here about two weeks, and he barely knows me.

"Private Washington," Miller begins, "I checked your personnel folder and noticed that you had worked for the Internal Revenue Service before you came into the army. What did you do?"

"I was a tax examiner in the Collection Division."

"Good. Our finance clerk is due to leave shortly, and his replacement hasn't arrived. You're going to be his replacement. Starting tomorrow, you are relieved from your MP duties. Report to Specialist Walsh in the Personnel Office in the morning."

I cannot believe my ears! Just like that, I am no longer an MP. No more sitting on the DMZ. No more taunting from the North Koreans. No more patrolling with that kid climbing up my back. I cannot be happier.

"Yes, sir," I say with a big grin on my face.

"Don't 'sir' me. I'm not an officer. Anyway, I thought it would make you happy to no longer have to work on the line," Miller says with a smile.

I GO BACK to my hooch (living quarters) and lie on my bunk, thinking of my good fortune and being unable to sleep. Snoring permeates the otherwise silent room. My fellow midnight-shift workers are fast asleep.

I think about my conversation with Specialist Walsh when he had processed my pay records on my first day on the compound. He was impressed by the fact that I got married after I was drafted and didn't use that as an excuse to avoid military service. Also, he found it odd that I ended up as an MP rather than in the clerical field with my background in civilian government service.

"Did you sign up for law enforcement as a possible occupation?" Walsh had asked.

"No. I guess someone surmised that working for the IRS was law enforcement. In a way it is—enforcing tax laws."

I suspect that Walsh had something to do with pointing me out as his possible replacement to the first sergeant.

I fall asleep, promising that I will write to Eve and tell her the good news when I awake this evening.

I PROMPTLY REPORT to Specialist Walsh in the morning. I had seen him earlier with friends at breakfast but kept my distance, not wanting to appear overly anxious. I do not tell anyone about my new assignment, including my fellow MPs. I do not know the process by which I was selected to be the company finance clerk, and I suspect that my being selected may generate some jealousy, animosity or competition. When my shift was getting ready to go on duty last night, I told them that the first sergeant had something for me to do in the morning.

"Congratulations," Walsh says as I sit down at his desk.

"Man, I really appreciate this! Performing guard duty up in the DMZ was going to make for a long year. I know that you had something to do with my being selected."

"Forget it. It was an easy choice. You're one of the smartest guys here. Besides, I have selfish reasons for recommending you. The quicker you learn my job, the sooner I will be able to go home. You know Specialist Wilson, our records clerk, over there?"

"Yeah."

"You will be working with him for a little while, but he's leaving too, within a month. We've verified that his replacement is on the way. I don't know what happened to mine. And, as you can see, we don't have a supervisor either. We've been waiting for that position to be filled too. I'm counting on you to learn your duties quickly because, as soon as we leave, you're going to be the most knowledgeable person in this office. There are 145 enlisted men and officers on this compound who are counting on you each month for their money and the money for their families. We cannot mess it up."

Suddenly I don't feel so lucky when I think of the awesome responsibility being placed on my shoulders.

"Rest assured that you can get plenty of help from the guys at I Corps in the payroll section. You must get the pay roster to them by the 20th of each month, so you have approximately 10 days until the end of each month to get it right. And, if for some reason some guy doesn't get paid, Captain Hall is always given extra money to issue an emergency pay voucher, if necessary. Try not to let that happen because you may have some explaining to do. Other than that, you'll be fine."

"Great," I say halfheartedly.

DURING THE NEXT few days, I try to learn all I can from Specialist Walsh before his departure. Luckily, a payday is coming up at the end of the month, so I can observe the routine with Walsh and Captain Hall.

Pay in the form of script is handed out in the mess hall. The men line up and, one by one, come to the table where we are sitting. They give their name and Specialist Walsh finds their pay statement. Then Captain Hall verifies the amount and counts it out to them. If the soldier raises a discrepancy, the finance clerk is there to address the problem. If the problem cannot be resolved on the spot, the GI is told to come to the Personnel Office later. It seems like the main problems revolve around the effective dates of promotions, demotions or allotments. Officers are paid later in the day, so their pay matters are not discussed in front of the enlisted men.

During the next few days, I work with Walsh to the point where he and I feel secure enough for him to leave. During this time, I process a couple of GIs into the JSA and prepare Walsh's pay records for departure.

One day before he leaves, Walsh asks me if I would be interested in his job of managing the library.

JSA Library

"It pays $50 a month," he explains, "but it is confining. The library hours are from 6:00 p.m. to 9:00 p.m. during the week and from noon to 9:00 p.m. on the weekends. You can always pay somebody to look after it if you want to go away for the weekend or take an evening off. The USO [United Service Organizations] office in Seoul maintains the library. A couple of ladies from the USO will periodically pay you a visit, bring new books and see if you are maintaining the library in good order. Also, the USO pays your salary."

"I'll take it," I say. "I only net about $72 a month salary, so an extra $50 a month will be great."

"Good. I'll recommend you for the job to Captain Hall and the USO staff."

THE PERSONNEL OFFICE is located within a metal gray Quonset hut similar to most of the other structures on the compound. Within the office are separate desks for the supervisory personnel sergeant, the finance clerk and the records clerk. Personnel records are contained in two US Army foot lockers, which can be closed instantly and put on a truck in case of a swift evacuation.

The office door swings open and the cool morning air flashes across my face.

Sergeant Michael Chestnut comes in and sits next to my desk. "Good morning, Private Washington. I need to see you about making a change to an allotment from my pay."

Sergeant Chestnut is a quiet, black man in his late 40s. His rank is E-7, which is just two steps below the highest rank attainable for an enlisted man. He has probably been in the army for much of his adult life. He is rather small in stature. His 5-foot 9-inch height is contrary to most other MPs assigned to the JSA.

Since being at the JSA, I learn that almost all the MPs assigned to the JSA are 6 feet tall or more, which is the US Army's way of trying to intimidate our smaller North Korean counterparts. This explains how I came to be here: My height kept me out of Vietnam.

Personnel Office

Chestnut is in charge of the MPs who perform security in the conference area. The US Army could not have found a better person to put on display for the North Koreans in spite of his height. He is immaculate in his dress. His uniform is perfectly creased and tailored to his well-chiseled body. His gold belt buckle sparkles, and his boots are shined to perfection. One can see why he was chosen for his position.

During his military service, Chestnut has served all over the world, including several previous tours of duty in Korea and one during the war. For some reason, I get the impression that he is proud of me working in an office position of significant importance, something that he probably had not seen too much of during his tenure in the army. After all, it's only been about 15 years since the US Armed Forces were integrated. Here I am—a young, black man, competently handling the financial matters for a whole unit.

"Okay, Sarge. I need you to fill out a new allotment form, indicating the changes you wish to make."

I hand him the form, and he starts to fill it out.

He notices the still-unoccupied supervisor's desk. "When is your new boss coming in?"

"I don't know. Hopefully, it will be soon."

"What's his name?"

"Let's see. Here it is. His name is Burton. Sergeant Andrew Burton."

Chestnut looks as if he has seen a ghost, and a strange look comes over his face. "Damn," he says under his breath. "There's going to be trouble."

I am curious, but he doesn't elaborate. Being only a private, I do not dare press him for more information before he leaves. Somehow, Sergeant Chestnut knows this guy, but I wonder how. Burton is an E-5, which means that he has probably been in the service for only a few years.

"Is it possible that Chestnut was stationed somewhere with this guy before?" I wonder.

Specialist Wilson's replacement arrives and is trained sufficiently so that Wilson is able to leave by the end of the month. The new records clerk is an 18-year-old private, also from Los Angeles, named Barry Harris.

OVER THE YEARS, the interior of the DMZ has grown thick with underbrush. Animals have flourished absent the presence of man. Occasionally, you can get a glimpse of a wild boar roaming in the wooded area off the road.

Also, the DMZ is very dangerous as there are mine fields, old artillery shells and war paraphernalia that neither side was permitted to remove once the truce was signed and the DMZ boundaries were established. No bulldozers, mine sweepers, tractors or other heavy equipment were allowed to clear the area.

Since the JSA is located in such an isolated area of Korea—away from the main population of the country as well as from other military installations—the army tries to provide the members of this unit with a number of activities to occupy idle time. There is an arts-and-crafts room equipped with a dark room for those interested in photography. The unit has a theater that shows movies all day on weekends. There are tennis courts, a baseball field, a library and a Noncommissioned Officers' (NCO) Club for enlisted men.

In addition, monthly Saturday night dances are held where girls from down south are brought in by bus. The young ladies, most of them prostitutes, are not allowed anywhere else on the compound except in the NCO Club. They are escorted by MPs from the bus to the front door of the club and then back to the bus when they leave. Most of the girls use the occasion to make future contacts for their business, although I sense that they enjoy dressing up and enjoying a night off from their profession.

Curiously, the army also allows some GIs, in their spare time, to hunt animals inside the DMZ with firearms like carbine rifles and shotguns.

BACK IN JANUARY—on my first day arriving at the JSA—one of the first GIs to befriend me in my hooch was Stephen Fisher (Specialist 4), an MP who had been in Korea for 10 months and was nearing the end of his tour. Stephen is Caucasian, 24 years old, heavyset and, like the rest of us, over 6 feet tall. He is a newlywed from Minnesota, and a picture of his lovely young wife Anna sits on the nightstand by his bunk. It looks like a picture she might have taken as a high school senior for her yearbook.

Stephen talks to me about not becoming depressed while living and working in such a highly intensive and volatile area. "Chris, if you're going to keep your sanity while you're here for a year, get involved in some meaningful activities during your spare time. You play sports?"

"Yeah. I played football at Fort Leonard Wood during basic training in Missouri. I've also played a little baseball and basketball."

"I played a little ball myself in high school and junior college—offensive tackle," Stephen says. "I went from the trenches of the football field to the trenches of the army."

"I played with some boys from Minnesota at Fort Leonard Wood," I add. "One of them had played a year or so at the University of Minnesota. They are some mean, tough dudes on the football field."

"Yeah, but I'm an old farm boy by nature. Playing football was something to do in school. I never thought I was very good at it. Besides, hunting and fishing are my things. The game I pursue in those activities doesn't hit back. You can play sports here. They hold tryouts for the football and basketball teams down south at the First Cavalry Division. If you make the team, the company will provide you time and transportation to the practice and the games."

"Thanks for the advice, Stephen. I'll look out for any bulletins regarding tryouts."

IT'S EARLY MORNING on the last day of February. I'm sitting in the barber's chair, getting a haircut before I go to work.

The compound barbershop is operated by an old Korean man whom everyone calls "Papa-san." He has two teenage daughters who work in the shop, helping to keep it clean and giving shoulder and neck massages at the completion of your haircut. The purpose of the massages is, hopefully, to illicit a favorable tip on top of the $2 haircut fee. Papa-san's daughters are the only Korean females allowed daily on the compound and are strictly "off limits." Everyone is warned not to say anything out of line to the girls; otherwise, you can be subject to disciplinary measures if caught doing so.

Papa-san speaks no English, so he gives everyone the same military-style haircut whether you are black, white, or whatever. Some GIs use other barbers in the villages, and some have their Korean girlfriends cut their hair. In any event, everyone is required to get a haircut every two weeks. A neat appearance is mandatory for those assigned to the JSA, although some of the "grease monkeys" who work in the motor pool don't seem to have to adhere to this requirement.

Papa-san turns the barber chair to a position where I can see the Arms Room out the window.

Two men are walking away in a jovial manner. One is Stephen Fisher, who has a shotgun broken down with the barrel pointing to the ground. The other is his friend Roger Watson, a fellow MP who has a carbine rifle strapped across his right shoulder. They are headed for the front gate, apparently going hunting in the wooded area outside the gate. They both came to the Personnel Office a few days ago, and we prepared their records for departure.

I think of how lucky they are to be going home. Apparently, they have nothing to do except wait for two days. Prior to leaving, GIs are relieved of duty and given two weeks to undergo a physical examination and get their affairs in order. Once the physical is completed, they are prohibited from leaving the compound. The army does not want anyone taking a venereal disease (VD) or other contagious disease back to the States.

PAPA-SAN FINISHES my haircut, and I get a neck massage from one of his daughters. I leave the barbershop and head down the path to the Personnel Office. It's a nice, cool, sunny morning, and I dread going into work.

In the office, Private Harris is talking to Sergeant Johnson, who is seated at his desk.

"Hey, Sarge," I say. "Don't tell me that you're leaving too?"

"Yeah, Chris, but I'll probably come back to Korea a time or two before my career is over. Hopefully not up here again."

Suddenly there is a loud explosion seemingly from nearby.

"Damn! What was that?" Harris murmurs.

Neither Johnson nor I respond. I think we are both waiting for a siren to go off to signal an invasion by the North Koreans. This is always in the back of your mind.

Nothing happens.

I break the silence. "I saw Fisher and Watson head for the front gate this morning. Looked like they were going hunting in the woods. I wonder if there was a shooting accident."

"That wasn't gunfire," the more seasoned sergeant chimed in. "Sounded more like a land mine going off."

An MP runs up to the colonel's office next door, screaming, "There's been an accident. A man has been injured in the woods. We need an ambulance."

Private Harris, Sergeant Johnson and I leave the office and run down to the front gate to see what has happened. From a distance, we see some very brave MPs quickly go into the woods to investigate. Apparently, about a hundred yards into the woods, Stephen had stepped on a land mine. The MPs put Stephen on a gurney and carry out his bloodied, mangled body. Watson was far enough away to avoid getting hit by the flying shrapnel.

The MPs take Stephen to the baseball field where the helicopter pad is located. Soon, a medical helicopter takes the injured soldier to the hospital. Stephen has unexpectedly found another foe who hit back.

I recall basic training and the discussion about land mines—or antipersonnel mines, as they are called. They are planted beneath the ground and have a sensitive fuse that can be set off by the weight of a small person; however, most animals do not weigh enough to trigger the device. To me, a land mine is a cowardly weapon. The enemy plants them in the ground, and then he is gone. He does not stay around to see who or how many people he has killed or injured. It may be hours, days or, in Stephen's case, years before he, the enemy, gets a hit.

BACK IN THE OFFICE, I ponder aloud, "Why would those two guys, who are so close to going home, take a chance going into those woods, knowing how dangerous it is in there? Was it stupidity, arrogance or simply boredom while trying to wait out the last two days? Who knows how many times they had gone in there before without incident?"

"They're idiots. That's all," Harris blurts out, quickly dismissing any philosophical reasons for their actions. The young guy fails to grasp the complexity of the situation. "You haven't spent 363 days up here like they have. The thought of sitting around for another two days was probably unbearable. They just fell back into doing something they like to do, something within their element. Who knows how we're going to handle it when it's our time to leave?"

THE ETHIOPIAN SOLDIER/
BURTON'S ARRIVAL

MILITARY PERSONNEL assigned to the JSA are part of the UN forces assigned to perform guard duty in the DMZ. The patch on our uniforms is the familiar blue-and-white world symbol with the encryption "United Nations Command Military Armistice Commission." Although the vast majority of the troops assigned to the JSA are American, there is a small contingent of soldiers from other countries, such as the dozen or so from Turkey and Ethiopia.

In conversation with some of the Ethiopian soldiers, I sadly learn that some of them have been here since the war ended. Man, the war ended in 1953, so that's at least 11 years ago … 11 years away from their home and family. They might as well have been in prison.

How the Ethiopian soldiers got here, I don't know, but their problem is how to get back to their country. I don't believe that Ethiopia has any commercial transportation between the two countries at this time. Surely the UN should get these men back to their home country, but that is not the case. Sadly, they still don't know when they're going home.

IT IS THE EVENING of March 17, 1964, and I am working in the library. An Ethiopian soldier named Omar comes in. He spends a lot of his free time in the library, reading or writing letters to his family.

"Good evening, Private Washington," he says in a polite and soft-spoken manner.

"What's happening, Omar? Heard from home lately?"

"Yes. I have new pictures of my children. You like to see?"

"Of course! Let me have a look."

"This is my son Asmar. This is my other son Joseph and my daughter Malek."

Omar is a very proud man and proud of his family. In his face, I see the loneliness and pain he has endured from the years of being separated from them. These precious pictures are, for all intents and purposes, his family.

Omar's children have dark hair, dark eyes and heavy, thick black eyebrows. They appear to be well into their teens. No doubt he has not seen them since they were toddlers.

"You have a nice family … very pretty children. You'll see them soon," I say, trying to offer words of encouragement.

"I hope so," he responds unconvincingly.

IT'S 7 A.M. on March 21—a nice, cool spring morning. The MPs are coming in from working the midnight shift in the DMZ and are turning in their weapons at the Arms Room. There is not much chatter among the tired, sleepy soldiers. They are in a hurry to go to the mess hall, eat breakfast and go to bed.

Guard duty in the DMZ is dangerous business, so the MPs carry live ammunition in case of attack. Before a weapon can be turned in, it must first be fired into a barrel of sand to ensure that no rounds are left in its chamber.

When I hear the crack of a .45-caliber pistol ring out in the quiet morning silence, the guys in the mess hall and I assume that some MP fired into the barrel of sand with a round of ammunition still in the chamber of his weapon.

Crack! A second round is discharged.

We all run outside to see what is going on at the Arms Room, which is about 50 yards away. In front of the barrel of sand, we see the fallen body of someone in an Ethiopian uniform. He is on his back with the gun laying loosely in his right hand. Parts of his head are splattered with blood in about a 4-foot trail, leading from the left side of his head. The soldier had shot himself in the right temple, but it took off the left side of his head.

I can see that the sprawled person on the ground is Omar.

"He missed the first time," a hysterical MP says. "His hand was shaking so bad that the first shot went over his head. Before I could get to him, he recocked and fired."

As I look at this dead, defeated soldier, I think that somewhere in his pocket are the pictures of his three fatherless children.

"I hope they know how much he loved them," I think. "I wish I had some way of telling them."

Someone places a sheet over Omar's body.

IT IS MARCH 26, 1964, and Captain Hall, Roger Watson and a few other buddies visit Stephen Fisher at the 8th Army hospital in Seoul. Watson's departure from Korea is delayed pending an investigation of the land-mine incident.

Later in the evening, in the mess hall, Watson describes his parting conversation with Stephen. Stephen knows that his legs have been amputated, but he thinks the doctors have not told him about the full extent of his injuries. Numb from medication, Stephen has no feeling in the lower part of his body. He asks Watson to stay behind for a minute after the others say their goodbyes and leave the room.

In a weak, trembling voice, Stephen tells Watson, "Lift my gown and let me know if I'm still a man."

Watson tells us that fear gripped him—the same fear that he felt in the mine field. He does not want to be the one to tell Stephen that his penis is gone. Why haven't the doctors told him the full story? Why is he going to have to be the one to tell him that he will never make love to his beautiful wife again?

Watson's hand is shaking as he reaches for the bottom of Stephen's gown. He decides not to prolong the agony, so he quickly lifts the gown, expecting to see some horrible form of disfigurement.

With a sigh of relief, he says, "Steve, old buddy, the way you're hung, you and Anna are going to have lots of children."

Stephen smiles and is at peace. "Come visit me if you're up around my parts in Minnesota. You've got my address."

"I will," Watson promises as he hugs him and says goodbye.

I think about Stephen's accident, the choices we sometimes make in life and the consequences that follow. Here, we have a situation where two young men survived a very dangerous environment for almost a year. Then, in one of their last two days, they make a bad decision that costs one man his legs and will profoundly affect both of them and their families for the rest of their lives.

WHEN SERGEANT BURTON arrives on March 10, he quickly finds out that the Personnel Office is in good hands with me handling the company's pay matters and Private Harris handling the personnel records. Burton spends all day in the office during his first week, but then his hours decline. He comes in for the first hour and then disappears to his hooch, presumably to drink. He becomes very fond of Harris and me. If anything important comes up, we know where to find him.

Burton is Caucasian, 48 years old, 6 feet 3 inches tall and about 195 pounds. His red nose and face expose his many years of alcohol abuse. Some evenings, when we go by his hooch after work to bring him up to date on the day's activities, we drink with him, although most of the time I beg off because of my evening job in the library.

I learn from Burton's personnel records that he was a highly decorated officer who had attained the rank of colonel after 17 years of distinguished service. He was awarded many medals including a Purple Heart for being wounded in military action. He wore "Wings," which are indicative of being a member of the paratroopers. All his combat action was in World War II. He had also served a tour in Korea, but it was not during the war.

Burton had been court-martialed and booted out of the army. A jury of five officers had found him guilty of "conduct unbecoming an officer and a gentleman." He was sentenced to three months in the brig and then dishonorably discharged from the service. He never mentioned the circumstances surrounding his demise in the army, but on one occasion he talked about his short plight in civilian life after his discharge.

ONE EVENING, during a drinking session, Harris asks Burton, "What did you do during the six months you were out of the army?"

Burton is lying across his bed with a drink in his hand. He is half-dressed in a green army undershirt and fatigue pants with green army socks on his feet. His dog tags dangle from his neck. This is probably the extent of his dress for today or yesterday.

I sit in a chair while Harris sits on the empty bunk opposite Burton. Normally, he should have another sergeant as a hooch mate, but no one seems to want to stay with him. Burton might be a drunk, but he respects military protocol and tradition. His living quarters are well kept; his military and civilian clothes hang neatly in his closet. He has no pictures of his wife or family, although he often speaks fondly of his wife, never having a bad word to say about her. I get the impression that she is a simple woman who somehow ended up marrying a very complicated man. Burton says that she quickly tired of the transient nature of military life early in their marriage, electing instead to stay home in Phoenix.

From the look on Burton's face, the thought of the six months in civilian life brings back painful memories.

"My father-in-law had me selling life insurance in Arizona," Burton begins. "I hated that shit. Selling insurance in that hot-ass desert was the most boring thing I'd ever done. I soon found myself talking to the army about how I could get back in."

He downs his drink and turns to his nightstand to pour another one.

After we leave Burton's hooch, I tell Harris, "Whatever happened to him, he's now trying to drown it in alcohol."

IT IS MARCH 27, 1964, at about 6 p.m. on Good Friday. I hurry up the path to the mess hall to try and eat dinner before closing time, and then go through the chow line quickly as there is no one else in line. The cook on duty, who is dishing out the food, is rather generous by giving me three pieces of fish, a hefty spoon of mashed potatoes and peas. He is probably trying to get rid of the surplus food he has cooked since many of the compound personnel have already gone off base for the holiday weekend. I guess he has to prepare enough food each day as if everyone is going to eat it.

"Come back, Chris, if you want more. I've got a lot left."

"Thanks, Cookie," I call to him, although his name is Clarence Martin, Sergeant E-5. It seems as if all the cooks in the army are called Cookie.

I make myself a salad in one of the wooden bowls alongside the salad tray, grab a couple of rolls and butter and get a soft drink from the beverage-dispensing machine.

When I first came into the mess hall, I noticed Sergeant Chestnut eating alone at a table in the back of the room.

"Mind if I join you?" I now ask as I approach his table.

It is not proper for a private to fraternize with higher ranked personnel, but I know these guys so well from dealing with their pay that I feel at ease talking to them.

"Please," he says, pointing to one of the chairs.

"Not going anywhere this holiday weekend?" I ask, knowing that this is a foolish question as Chestnut rarely leaves the compound.

"No. Gotta work this weekend."

"I bet he volunteered," I think as I pick at Cookie's tasteless food.

Chestnut's dark skin is smooth and flawless. He is clean shaven, and his hair is neatly trimmed. It is 6 p.m., and he looks like he has just gotten dressed. This man is a poster child for the army.

I ask, "Are you working the late shift?"

"No. I just got off."

"Incredible," I think again.

"How's your new boss working out?" he asks, staring innocently at his plate of food.

"He's an interesting fellow. He's quiet and stays to himself. He pretty much lets Harris and me run the Personnel Office. He trusts us to do our jobs."

"Great. His drinking is not a problem?"

I am not about to touch that one. "The guy knows his stuff. He's there when we need him." Quickly changing the subject, I add, "How did you come to know him?"

I had wanted to ask Sergeant Chestnut this question for weeks and now finally have the opportunity. It was one reason that I decided to sit with him when I came into the mess hall.

"I was stationed at Fort Lewis, Washington, when Burton came back into the service in 1959," Chestnut explains. "I'm sure you know by now that he was once a full-bird colonel—one promotion away from becoming a general."

"Yeah. I gathered as much from conversations with him and from his personnel records."

I must have caught Chestnut on a good day because he is willing to talk.

"The word around Fort Lewis was that Burton had been court-martialed out of the army for an adulterous affair he had with his commanding officer's wife," he continues. "I believe this happened in 1958 when he was serving as an assistant to the commandant of the base at Fort Ord, California. I think his name was Nielsen. Yeah, Brigadier General Raymond Nielsen. Serving as Nielsen's assistant, he probably performed a number of duties, least of which was to arrange social functions on behalf of the general."

"Man, he must have been nuts to mess around with a general's wife."

"No one knew exactly how long the affair had been going on. Burton had worked for the general for several years, so he and Mrs. Nielsen probably had ample time to get to know each other. I'm sure he was a frequent visitor to the Nielsen home, arranging formal dinner parties and such."

"How did he get back into the service?"

"You know, that's a mystery. Word is that he still has important friends in Washington who made it happen. The guy had been in the army for 17 years, just three years short of being eligible for retirement. Somehow, he was let back in to get the final three years with the condition that he come back as a private. He has gotten the three years and worked his way back up to E-5. He could have retired by now, but I guess the army is his life."

"He came back as a private? What was that like?"

"Brutal. Have you heard the saying, 'Be careful how you treat people on the way up because you might meet them again on the way down'? Well, he met them again after he was down."

"What do you mean?"

"At Fort Lewis, Burton ran into some of those same people he had stepped on. He got his payback as a private."

"What did they do to him?"

"He got every shitty detail possible. You know, like excessive KP, picking up trash, policing the company area and cleaning toilets and the grease pit."

Cleaning the grease pit is a job that everyone hates because you invariably get filthy and are covered in grease. Army mess halls use a lot of oil, which is dumped into a pit in the ground outside. Periodically, the pit has to be emptied and the grease removed. Once full, the 3-foot deep, 4-foot by 4-foot pit has to be emptied by scooping out the grease and putting it into containers for pickup. Then, somebody has to get into the pit and scrub it clean.

"Seeing a once-mighty colonel in that pit must have been a sight to behold," I say. "I bet the enlisted men got a kick out that."

"Yes, but he took it. He took the humiliation, the degradation and the embarrassment. He took it like a man, never complaining, as if to punish himself for a grave mistake that he made in life.

"Then things changed. Slowly he began to earn the respect of his fellow enlisted men. He became a personnel clerk. Like you, he was in contact with everyone in his company. He knew the army backward and forward and became a jailhouse lawyer, so to speak. Officers hated him because of his knowledge of military protocol. Many of the enlisted men came to him for advice about things like being overlooked for promotion, excessive discipline and officer misconduct. The guy became a hero and a legend in the army. There probably is not one military base in the world where someone has not heard the tale of Colonel Andrew Burton, aka Private Andrew Burton."

For a second, I think that even Chestnut has become an admirer of this man—although he has probably never broken an army rule in his life or filed a complaint about anything.

"Man, I had no idea what he's been through. He must be one tough dude."

Chestnut picks up his tray and begins to leave the table with one last parting shot. "Yeah, until you factor in the alcoholism. Then you think that maybe he's not so tough after all."

KOREAN GIRL

DURING MY FIRST FEW months in Korea, I rarely ventured into the nearby Korean villages south of the bridge where GIs hung out in local bars and prostitution was rampant. I took Stephen Fisher's advice and became involved in a number of meaningful activities.

First, I took over the job of managing the compound library in the evening and on weekends. The library is under the auspices of the USO club headquartered in Seoul. I would receive periodic visits from ladies from the USO whose job it was to make sure the library was being maintained properly. I would have enjoyed the pleasure of the company of these American females except they would give me hell for the condition in which they sometimes found the library. Books were not always reshelved in a timely manner, and I was sometimes slow in cataloging, labeling and shelving new books that had been shipped to me.

Second, I tried out for the First Cavalry basketball team. Although basketball was never really my sport, I made the team, which probably can be attributed more to my athleticism than my basketball skills. Basketball practices and games were held in Seoul, so for a while I spent a lot of evenings and weekends away from the JSA. I would pay Private Harris or John Gibson to cover for me in the library when I was away playing ball.

The basketball season was kind of spotty because games were frequently postponed or cancelled, mainly because of civil unrest in the country that would result in restricted US military travel. I recall helping win one game for my team when I hit a jump shot from the top of the key (the free-throw lane) to beat an American high school team located in Seoul. These were kids of military and civilian personnel who worked in South Korea. Our team was successful in winning our league and, at the end of the season in March, our team fared well, coming in third place in the First Cavalry division championships.

Being involved in sports, my librarian job and other company activities, I quickly became well respected and admired among my peers and officers. Also, it was well known that I did not frequent *yong sekshis* (prostitutes in the nearby villages). Thus far, in April, I had been true to the pact that John Gibson and I had made at Fort Gordon, Georgia (i.e., that we would be true to our wives while away from home in this foreign country).

Another example of my popularity was shown by the fact that I was selected to be the company flag bearer during all formal ceremonies. In addition, sometimes Captain Hall would ask me to play doubles with him in tennis whenever he needed a partner while entertaining visiting dignitaries. Here again, I was just a marginal tennis player, but I was polite, respectful and knew how to conduct myself among officers. I would never argue whether an opponent's ball was in or out but would rather leave such challenges to Captain Hall.

I HAVE BEEN PROMOTED to private first class, so I am finally able to have stripes on my uniform and no longer be a private, which is the lowest rank in the army. My Korean houseboy Kim quickly sews my stripes on all my uniforms. It seems like everyone in the country is named either Kim or Lee—probably tantamount to the common names Smith and Johnson in the States.

On the Saturday after I am promoted, I go to the PX at Camp Casey to buy toiletries, candy, cigarettes and a few other things. Prior to leaving the compound, one first has to go to the duty officer (D/O) to receive clearance and obtain a pass to get on the bus. Sometimes GIs are restricted from leaving the compound for various reasons such as disciplinary actions, medical issues like a VD or—in the case of Stephen Fisher and Roger Watson—orders to go home. The D/O, who normally is not an officer but rather a sergeant, will have a list of those individuals restricted to the compound.

THIS MORNING, Sergeant Raymond Liggins is on duty when I stop by to get a pass. Liggins is one of the supervisory MPs I worked for when I first arrived at the JSA.

He notices the new private-first-class stripes on my uniform. "Congratulations! I see that you've been promoted."

"Yeah. Now I am going into town to spend some of my big money."

"Not on girls, I hope. But, if you do, you'd better take some of these," he says, pointing to a basket full of condoms.

One of the D/O's jobs is to counsel GIs who are leaving the compound on the need to practice safe sex.

"Did you hear that poor bastard agonizing in the latrine the other night?" Liggins asks me. "You could hear him all over the compound. He was trying to pee through a penis whose head was probably the size of a baseball. He had to learn his lesson the hard way."

"Who was that?"

"One of those motor-pool guys. He went on sick call the next morning."

"I'll pass on the condoms. I'm going shopping at the PX. Not interested in the local girls," I say as I pick up my pass and walk out the door.

THE BUS ARRIVES at the front gate of Camp Casey at about 10:30 a.m. I decide to stroll the streets of Yong Ju Gol for a little while before going to the PX. I want a hamburger, but it is too early to eat. Also, I do not want to carry around the items I am going to buy from the PX until I am ready to go back to the compound.

The center of the village of Yong Ju Gol is a dirt road with small shops lining each side of the street for about three city blocks. Small pools of water stand intermittently in the middle of the street—probably from merchants pitching water out the front door of their establishments. This village has no indoor plumbing, which makes for some very unsanitary conditions. Water runs in ditches under the dirt sidewalks, probably draining into the rice paddy fields behind the town. Rats the size of cats scurry about the village. A few GIs and natives slowly meander down the center of the street.

I wander around, peering into the windows of the many shops and looking for nothing in particular. I see a photography studio and consider going in to have some pictures taken to send home to my family, showing the new stripes on my uniform.

As I look through the window, I see the photographer frantically trying to get a young Korean girl to smile as she poses for a picture. About 20-something years old, the girl is seated in a chair, facing the window with a backdrop of a dark, velvet curtain behind her. She is wearing a beautiful, white, short-sleeved dress and white sandals.

She glances at me and, for some reason, I decide to help out the photographer. I turn my hat sideways, cross my eyes and make a funny face, trying to get her to smile. A big grin appears on her face as the shutter opens and the lights from the photographer's camera go off. He gets his picture.

I laugh, straighten my hat and start to walk away from the window. Still frozen in her posed position, I notice her right hand push toward the floor as if to indicate to me to stop and wait until she is through. I light a cigarette and decide to wait for her.

AS I SMOKE a cigarette, I look down the street. I can see some of the working girls slowly come out of their respective clubs and solicit GIs to come in. Saturday is probably one of their most profitable days, so they are starting early.

From conversations I've overheard in the library and from reading materials, I have learned that Korean prostitutes are not allowed to walk the streets but rather have to be discreet and work out of hospitality clubs for a house madam or, in the alternative, work out of their own shack or apartment.

Prostitution is legal in this country as these working women are considered patriots, performing a needed service for the ROK. The girls are required to have weekly examinations for VDs at the many medical clinics such as "Dr. Pak's Love Clinic No. 1," "Dr. Oh's Clinic No. 5" or "Mr. Lee's Clinic No. 3." They wear a picture identification card around their neck, showing the date of their last examination. Any girl found to have a VD is banished to places called "monkey houses" until they are cured. Sometimes the cure can take months, which can be devastating to the girl's family income. That is why so many of them who suspect that they have a VD avoid the medical checkups and keep working underground. Hence, you have sad cases like the motor-pool guy in the latrine who happened to find one of those untested women.

Main street of Yong Ju Gol

THE YOUNG GIRL finishes with the photographer and comes outside. Again, she has the same serious look on her face that the photographer was trying to erase.

In very broken English, she says, "Me no whore."

She wants that fact understood right from the start. I can tell from her appearance that she is not one, even without a plastic card around her neck.

"Me not looking for one," I reply.

Again, I get her to smile.

"My name Mi Chung Kim."

"Oh, great," I think. "Another Kim."

"No," I say, pointing to her. "Your name Mi No Whore. That's what you told me."

She laughs as she looks up, trying to see the name plate on the right side of my chest.

"Washington," I say, slowly trying to pronounce it for her. "Glad to meet you," I add as I take off my hat and bow to her.

We start to walk down the center of the street in the direction of Camp Casey's main gate. I totally forget about my taking a picture to send back home.

"Where you work?" she asks in broken English.

"Panmunjom."

It seems as though every person in the country is trying to learn English. She has probably never seen the blue-and-white UN patch on my shoulder since there are only about 145 of us GIs assigned to the UNC. The vast majority of the 31,000 American troops in Korea is assigned to the First Cavalry division whose patch is bright yellow with a horse's head in black.

I see the surprised look on her face. She knows that the city of Panmunjom is in North Korea.

"The DMZ. The Demilitarized Zone, north of the Imjin River," I quickly add.

"Oh," she nods.

I point to the main gate of Camp Casey and make a gesture with my hands as if eating. I indicate that I want her to come along.

She agrees.

KOREAN NATIVES are not allowed on US military bases unless they work there, but the PX, movie theater and restaurant are situated in such a way that GIs can bring guests to those facilities. Rarely are any of the working girls invited onto the base by their GI customers.

On the way to the gate, we stroll past the Club Moulin Rouge.

A female voice yells, "Washington-san, she's not a whore. You come back see me. I f*** you good. Show you good time."

"Shit," I think.

I can see the disappointment on Mi Chung's face as she realizes that one of the girls knows me by name. It is a girl name Mona, who comes to the Saturday night dances at our NCO Club. The Korean prostitutes give themselves short, easy names—Mona, Linda, Suzi and Mary—for their GI customers to remember.

Mona and a lot of the girls like to dance with me because I am a good dancer. I enjoy dancing with them too. I learned to dance as a teenager while hanging out at high-school dances with my older sister and her girlfriends. Sometimes I had to dance with three or four girls at one time and, in Korea, it is no different. There are very few guys in the military who really know how to dance.

Mi Chung sneers at Mona. It appears as though they know each other. At least Mona knows that Mi Chung is not one of the girls. I wish that I can explain to Mi Chung how these girls know me. However, right now, my Korean and her English are not good enough for an explanation, and I feel no obligation to give her one anyway. After all, I only met her about 15 minutes ago.

I am curious about Mona because Private Harris considers her his girlfriend. She knows that we are coworkers and friends, so why would she solicit me? I suspect jealousy because I am leading Mi Chung in the direction of Camp Casey.

Mona is dressed in a tank top and a mini skirt. Her inch-long fingernails are painted bloody red. She is a little bit taller than most Korean girls. She may have been half white, half Korean—what the Koreans call *tweggis* (mixed races). She is wearing heavy makeup, so it is hard to tell. She is cute.

I think, "If I were to screw one of these whores, she would be the one."

She is far and away the most attractive of the girls working the *gomshis* (black) side of the street. Yes, even in this foreign country, even in this little dirty village, *gomshis* and *miguks* (whites) are segregated. Certain clubs are patronized by blacks and others by whites. Korean men are prohibited from going into these hospitality clubs.

MI CHUNG AND I eventually make it to Camp Casey's restaurant and sit opposite each other in a booth. The restaurant is like a typical American diner with booths around the wall, a few tables and chairs in the center and stools at the counter. The short-order cook, who can be seen through the square opening to the kitchen, is American.

I think, "He is probably a GI, working part-time similar to my job in the library."

Our waitress is a Korean woman who speaks very good English. Her name tag says, "Betty." She brings us water and two menus.

"I'll be back to take your order," she says.

The menus are in English, so Mi Chung has no idea what she is looking at. When Betty comes back, I ask her to explain the menu to Mi Chung. That does not help because she is not familiar with nor does she have a taste for American food.

"Me not want anything," Mi Chung says.

I tell Betty, "I'll have a cheeseburger with mayonnaise, lettuce, tomatoes, fries and a Coke. Bring my friend a vanilla malt."

I think, "Everybody loves sweets, no matter what their nationality is."

Mi Chung is not overly attractive, but there is a sweet, clean freshness about her compared to the other Korean women I have been exposed to (i.e., working girls from the hospitality clubs).

When Betty returns with the food, Mi Chung says something to her in Korean.

"She wants you to know that she is from a small village near Pusan," Betty explains, "and that she is here for a few weeks visiting her sick aunt, who lives down the alley from the Club Moulin Rouge."

"Thanks, Betty."

I start to eat my burger and then motion for Mi Chung to take a French fry. "Try one."

She does but, from the look on her face, the taste is totally foreign. She eats one fry and quickly takes a sip of her malt.

"You like that better," I add, pointing to her malt.

She smiles and nods.

She is content to watch me as I eat. She studies me intensely. I get the impression that I am a novelty to her as she probably has never been this close to a black man before.

I wonder, "What is going through her mind? Is she comparing me to other Americans or other Korean boys whom she has known? What has she learned about American blacks from TV and magazines? Is she asking herself why American whites want to segregate themselves from these people at home although they live and work together in the army?"

"What are you thinking?" I ask her, pointing to my temple.

"Why you eat fast?"

I have to laugh because I am reading more into her curiosity than there really is. "My cheeseburger is good. I haven't had one since I left home."

"How long Korea?"

"Four months."

The restaurant is beginning to fill up with customers. Several tables are occupied by groups of GIs, and one GI eats alone. A few booths are occupied by other couples including an American soldier with a Korean woman.

I NOTICE a young, white guy named Buddy Davis from my unit, sitting on the same side of the booth with his girlfriend Gina (one of the working girls). He also sits with her in a similar manner at the Saturday night dances, attached to her like a clinging vine. She is probably his first love.

When I came to the village this morning, I sat across from Buddy on the bus. He told me that his tour of duty would soon be coming to an end and that he was going to petition the US military to marry Gina and take her with him. I guess a military person needs the army's permission to marry a foreigner. To many of the Korean whores, the only way out of their bleak situation is to get lucky and have a soldier marry them and take them to America. To them, it is like hitting a home run in baseball.

On the bus, I asked Buddy, "What are you going to do if the army denies your request to marry?"

"Man, I don't know. If they deny my request, then I guess I'll try to extend my tour of duty. I don't want to leave Gina."

"Can you do that? Can you extend beyond 12 months?"

"I don't know, but I'll try."

I stared out the bus window at the rows and rows of rice paddies and the farmers trying to scratch out a living from their meager crops.

I think, "This guy must be nuts if he would rather stay here than go home."

Then, I think, "How ironic for me, a black man, to still think that anyone would be better off at home in America. America—where there are violent, ugly, civil-rights demonstrations. An America filled with bigotry and hatred. An America that just killed its leader. An America that is beginning to violently protest its government's involvement in the Vietnam War. Maybe I'm the one who is nuts to want to go back while all of that is going on."

At the restaurant, I nod to Davis, and he acknowledges my greeting with a big grin. He is in another world when he is with his girl.

MI CHUNG HAS drunk about half of her malt, but it is too much for her to finish. I eat the last of the French fries on my plate and signal to Betty for the check. I need to get back to the compound to relieve Harris, who is covering for me in the library. Since this is Saturday, he probably wants to come into the village later tonight and hook up with Mona.

When Betty brings the check, I ask her to explain to Mi Chung that I have to get back to my compound to go to work, but I will first walk her back to her aunt's house. I pay the check and leave Betty a generous tip for her help in interpreting for me. As we leave the restaurant, we pass by the movie theater, and Mi Chung stops to stare in amazement at the billboards advertising the current and upcoming films.

"Would you like to see one of these American movies with me one day?" I ask, pointing at her and myself.

Her eyes light up. "Yes!"

"Okay," I say, "but, in exchange, you must help me learn about your country."

"You want know Korea?"

"Yes," I respond as we begin our walk back to the village. "I would like to see some of the historical sites in Seoul."

She looks puzzled—probably because she doesn't understand the words "historical" and "sites."

I add, "I want to see places like Pagoda Palace, Gyeongbokgung Palace and Changgyeong Zoo."

"Ah," she nods, seemingly surprised that I know the names of those places.

With so much time on my hands while working in the library, I learned a little bit about South Korea. Also, some of the GIs in my unit, who had been in Korea for a while, had done some sightseeing and taken pictures of some of these historical places. I think it might be neat to see them with a Korean native and with someone to help me get around the city. At least that is my initial intention with Mi Chung as I have no romantic interest in her at this time.

Her interest in me is another story, however.

Black Alley

WE WALK DOWN an alley, which is called Black Alley because it is frequented by black GIs, until we come to her aunt's grass shack. She signals for me to wait a minute while she goes inside the flimsy door. A few minutes later, she comes out with a little Korean lady whom I assume is her aunt. The lady is very thin and frail and dressed in clothing similar to many of the women I see bent over and working in the rows and rows of rice paddies. She too has probably spent many years in those rice paddies, and that labor has taken a toll on her body.

Mi Chung speaks to her aunt in Korean, telling her my name and who I am and that I had taken her to eat at the American compound.

The little lady smiles warmly and bows as she reaches out to me with her weak, trembling hand. I get the impression that she is pleased that her niece has met someone—an American GI.

I bow to her as I take her hand and say hello.

She motions to Mi Chung and me to come inside.

"No, thank you. I have to go," I answer. I turn to Mi Chung and say, "I'll come by and see you again the next time I'm in the village."

She grabs my arm as if to ask, "When?"

"In a few days. I'll be back," I promise as I walk down the alley toward the main street.

JSA ANNIVERSARY/AMERICAN PRISONERS RETURNED

IT'S TUESDAY, MAY 5, 1964—Cinco de Mayo at home, but we're celebrating the 12th anniversary of the activation of our Support Group. It's a pleasant, sunny morning, about 70 degrees F. Everyone is dressed casually in jeans or shorts and T-shirts. The company falls into formation at 10 a.m. in the picnic area, just outside the front gate and near the helicopter pad. Most of the officers and enlisted men are present except for those on duty.

Major General Charles Nelson of the UNC Military Armistice Commission is addressing the assembled group: "Lieutenant Colonel Richmond, on this, the occasion of the 12th anniversary of the activation of your organization on 5 May 1952, I wish to take this opportunity to congratulate you, your officers and enlisted men on the splendid record of accomplishments of the United States Army Support Group, Joint Security Area, in the pursuit of its vital and most unique mission."

The major general is a tall, Caucasian man, about 50 years old, approximately 6 feet tall with mixed-gray hair. He has been highly decorated as evidenced by the numerous medals and ribbons displayed on the upper left chest area of his uniform. The two silver stars on each shoulder glisten in the early morning sunlight. The two-star general is the senior member of the UN Delegation, which holds meetings with the North Koreans.

He continues. "Over the years, your unit has continued to distinguish itself as a proud, well-disciplined and highly professional organization, capable of performing all assigned tasks with exceptional efficiency and dispatch. On behalf of the United Nations Command Military Armistice Commission, I wish all of you continued success in the tradition established by your predecessors and which you are all continuing in such an outstanding manner. Thank you and enjoy your Organization Day."

Standing here, holding the American flag as flag bearer, I am overwhelmed with emotion and filled with pride while listening to the major general's comments. Suddenly, I realize that I am part of something much bigger than just a group of guys providing guard duty in the JSA. A tradition has been established, and there are predecessors—guys who have walked this path many times before us. I can only imagine what the anxiety, fear and uncertainty was like for those brave souls who had to perform their duty that first year immediately after the ceasefire. That must have been even more nerve-racking, knowing that hostilities had just ended but could start all over again at any minute.

The company lets out a loud yell, and Captain Hall dismisses us so we can start an enjoyable day of activities that include softball and volleyball games and horseshoes.

Teams are formed for the various games as follows:

- Officers and senior NCOs vs. MP Group #1
- Signal Corps vs. Headquarters Personnel
- Transportation vs. MP Group #2

The KATUSA and foreign soldiers are taking part, playing with teams from their assigned sections.

Private First Class John "Alphabet" Papangelopoulos, who is on duty in the Signal Corps unit, comes on the public-address system and says, "After the sports activities, lunch will be served in the mess hall at noon and then a Beer Bust at 1 p.m. The day will conclude after dinner with Dance Night beginning at 1800 hours [6 p.m.] in the NCO Club."

Organization Day

MILITARY AND CIVILIAN personnel can visit and observe the conference building where talks with the North Koreans are held. Visitors can observe the conferences by standing outside the building and looking through windows provided for spectators. While thousands of guests visit the area from the south, the communist side permits relatively few—mainly Chinese visitors from mainland China.

I have visited the conference area a few times while off duty when the talks where in session. I found that nothing much comes out of them except finger-pointing and accusations by each side, so most visitors use the occasion for picture-taking and an opportunity to observe the North Korean soldiers up close. It has been a while since I took time to go to the conference area, but gossip is circulating on the compound that there may be an upcoming session worth a visit.

PRIVATE FIRST CLASS Louis Lancaster is the secretary for Lieutenant Colonel Richmond, whose office is directly opposite the Personnel Office, about 50 feet between the two offices. Lancaster is a 20-year-old male Caucasian, thin and frail and gay but still in the closet. Although Richmond is the commanding officer of the JSA, he generally allows Captain Hall to run the day-to-day operations of our Support Group, mainly dealing with dignitaries and matters affecting the UNC Armistice Commission. Most days, Lancaster is alone in his office, so he spends a lot of time visiting with us in the Personnel Office.

At 9 a.m. on May 15, Lancaster comes through the door of the Personnel Office and sits in a chair next to Sergeant Burton's desk. As usual, Burton has not made it to the office. I'm working at my desk, and Harris is drinking a cup of coffee, smoking a cigarette and reading the newspaper. Neither of us acknowledges Lancaster's presence since we all live in the same hooch and just left each other less than an hour ago.

I can tell that Lancaster is dying to tell us something important, but I act uninterested. Normally, he does not come over this early, so I assume that Lieutenant Colonel Richmond has not come into his office yet. However, Lancaster has received a message for the colonel, which he eager to share with us.

"The Armistice Commission is holding a meeting on Saturday," Lancaster says to no one in particular.

Neither Harris nor I respond. We know that whatever he is going to tell us will come out eventually.

Lancaster continues. "I think we should go to this one."

"Why?" Harris says angrily, finally putting down his paper and acknowledging Lancaster's presence. "Are those asshole North Koreans finally going to end the standoff?" he asks sarcastically.

Ignoring Harris's question, Lancaster leans over in a hushed manner. "Word is the North Koreans are going to return two American helicopter pilots who were shot down and captured about a year ago."

Lancaster now has my attention. "That's news because heretofore the North Koreans have never acknowledged at prior meetings that the pilots were still alive. I'm going. I want to see what condition these guys are in."

THE TEMPERATURE is well above 90 degrees F on Saturday morning, May 18, 1964. I am wearing my short-sleeved khaki uniform, but it is still uncomfortable on the bus traveling up to the conference area. I'm with my buddy John Gibson whom I know from our days at MP school at Fort Gordon, Georgia. John finally arrived at the JSA in early February, about a month after I got here. Instead of reporting to the Oakland Debarkation Center in January like I did, he foolishly went back to Fort Gordon after the Christmas holidays, unsuccessfully trying to get reassigned in the States in order to stay with his wife. The man is truly in love.

"What do you think these guys will look like?" he asks me.

"Heck, I don't know. The North Koreans have not even said if they're alive. If they are alive, they may have been injured in the helicopter crash and not received medical attention. And they may have been tortured."

The bus pulls into the conference area at 9:30 a.m., about a half hour before the scheduled meeting. We walk to the observation windows of the conference building and look in, but there is no activity inside.

A contingent of US military dignitaries emerges from a door on the UN side of the building, and a similar group can be seen from the Communist side. Everyone is standing around, but it appears that no one knows why because neither side is saying anything to the other.

There are about 100 spectators consisting of US military personnel and civilians. Most of the civilians appear to be reporters from South Korea. Others in the attentive gallery are North Koreans soldiers who appear to be just as intrigued by this whole episode as we are. At this moment, we are interested spectators oblivious to the confrontational nature of our relationship.

We all look north and see a cloud of dusk being kicked up by a black limousine, which has just crossed the Bridge of No Return from the northern side. During the short time I worked as an MP here, I never saw vehicles other than trucks come across the bridge. Now, seeing an automobile from the north made the North Koreans seem more civilized and nonthreatening. As the black car pulls into the conference area, I see that it is a Mercedes-Benz.

"These Communists pulling up here in a Benz looks like they're trying to make a statement about their wealth and prosperity. What a joke," I whisper to John.

Two North Korean officers get out of the car and speak briefly with their counterparts and then to the US military contingent. The back door of the limousine opens and two prisoners, who are surrounded by North Korean guards, slowly step out. An American officer is allowed to approach the two pilots, shake their hands and say, "Welcome back."

A photographer from the *Stars and Stripes* newspaper, who is standing on something that resembles a box, towers over the group and rapidly takes pictures. Another Korean reporter scribbles notes on his notepad as a cigarette dangles from his lips. Then another reporter stares intently at the proceedings without writing on his pad.

"Did he witness this scene about 13 years ago when these two combatant nations exchanged 20,000 prisoners of war at the Bridge of No Return?" I silently wonder.

THE TWO PRISONERS, who are dressed in drab gray Communist prison uniforms, are Captains Bruce Thomas and Clarence Scott. They have recent haircuts that are closely cropped around their ears. Although in their 30s, they look about 50 years old.

Stars & Stripes *newspaper: American prisoners*

American prisoners

Before the pilots are turned over to our side, and as a condition for their release, an American officer reads a statement admitting to conducting espionage activities along the DMZ. Satisfied with the public admission of violating the truce agreement, the North Koreans allow our MPs to come forward and take possession of the two men. Sergeant Chestnut, Captain Hall and a squad of 12 MPs march into the area and surround the pilots.

The American MPs tower over their smaller North Korean counterparts. The letters "MP" are emblazoned in bold white letters on their black helmets and armbands. They are dressed in well-tailored, short-sleeved khaki uniforms with white-belt and white-glove accessories. They are wearing white scarfs around their necks, neatly tucked under the open collars of their shirts, with .45-caliber revolvers holstered in their belts. They make a colorful sight.

By comparison, the North Korean soldiers are dressed in dull green uniforms consisting of baggy coats and pants, presumably to show an abundance of material resources in their country. Their weapons are holstered in leather belts around their waists, which are connected to other straps that run diagonally across their right shoulders. Their green armbands have the letter "O" on top of the letter "T," which apparently is the Korean equivalent of "MP." I imagine that wearing those uniforms must be brutal in this heat.

John comments about the lack of emotion or jubilation displayed by the two American pilots.

"We don't know the circumstances surrounding their capture," I say. "Did they screw up by flying too close to the North Korean border? Maybe they think they might be facing a court-martial because of the embarrassment they caused to the United States. Who knows what admissions they may have made to the Communists. I can think of a lot of reasons why they aren't smiling."

After the pilots' release, they are driven back to our compound where they quickly change into US military uniforms and, ironically, board a military helicopter for the 20-minute flight to the 8th Army hospital in Seoul for physical examinations.

A North Korean officer reads a statement before turning over American prisoners.

IT IS THE Monday morning after my visit to the conference area. I am at my desk, drinking a cup of coffee and reading the latest news in *Stars and Stripes*. Sergeant Burton is at his desk, which is rare for a Monday morning.

News from home mainly involves ongoing presidential primary elections: Governor Nelson Rockefeller of New York wins the Oregon Republican Primary against his main competitors Barry Goldwater and Richard Nixon. President Lyndon Johnson is running unopposed on the Democratic side. Alabama Governor George Wallace is running as an Independent. Although Rockefeller won the Oregon primary, it looks as though he stands little chance of winning the Republican nomination this November. The newspaper also gives an account of the circumstances surrounding the two pilots' release.

I laugh. "The paper says that a UN spokesman recanted his admission of espionage, calling it meaningless. He said that the two pilots were just out on a routine mission, checking border markings, when they were shot down."

Burton, showing his keen awareness of military intelligence and knowledge of what's going on around us, chimes in. "I suspect they were doing more than checking signs. The US Army believes that about 70 percent of North Korea's million-plus army is stationed within about 62 miles of the DMZ, so I'm sure we want to keep a close eye on their movement and activities. What I don't understand is why spy in something as vulnerable as a helicopter?"

The newspaper goes on to say that, after the pilots' physical examinations, which disclosed both men in good health, they were allowed to make telephone calls to their families. Captain Thomas was the first to get through to his wife and their three small boys. Captain Scott had trouble getting through to his wife, but she was subsequently located, and he was able to talk to her and their five-year-old son.

I think of how lucky these four young American boys are to have their fathers. Although they lost contact for over a year, they will most likely grow up with long and loving relationships. Somewhere in another part of the world, three young Ethiopian children will not have that same opportunity.

DANGERS OF THE DMZ

IT'S FRIDAY EVENING on June 12, 1964. After Papa-san (the compound barber) cuts my hair, I head up the path from the barbershop to the mess hall for dinner. The weather is absolutely perfect this time of year as spring turns to summer.

"Maybe I'll go to Seoul for the weekend," I think, "if I can find someone to cover for me in the library. In the morning, I'll get up early and catch the 9 a.m. bus out of the compound and head for Seoul."

I fall asleep, eagerly anticipating my trip to Seoul in the morning.

AT 3 A.M., I am awakened by a blast of a horn coming from the company loudspeaker. I rub my eyes and sit up in my bunk, trying to clear the fog and comprehend the noise. Then I hear another three blasts and the lights come on.

"Damn!" I say out loud as others begin to wake up. "That means evacuate. Shit! Get up and get dressed," I yell to nobody in particular.

I put on my clothes and nervously sit on the side of my bunk, lacing up my boots. My hands are trembling. I'm trying to remember our evacuation procedures, which we go over at least once a month. Sheer fear and panic grip my thoughts.

"Are the North Koreans invading?" I wonder. "Are we going to be able to make it across the bridge before they get here? Am I going to die? Is this it? Why did this have to happen while I am here?"

Suddenly, Sergeant Burton comes through the door.

"Move it!" he yells. "Get to the Arms Room, get your weapon and report to your respective assignments."

Burton is fully dressed, with a combat pack on his back and a .45-caliber pistol on his right hip. He looks military and ready for combat. He's demonstrating leadership. Suddenly, my fear is gone, and I find myself following his orders.

I yell to Harris, "Come on. Let's go!"

OUR ASSIGNED WEAPON is a .30-caliber machine gun, which we are required to clean on a weekly basis. Harris and I just cleaned our weapons yesterday, and we joked about not knowing how to fire the damn thing if we ever had to do so.

About 30 anxious GIs line up in front of us at the Arms Room, trying to retrieve their weapons from two frustrated soldiers who are working frantically behind the counter. Some of the comments being screamed at the two men are "Come on up there!" and "This is ridiculous!"

Harris and I finally reach the counter.

"Cal 30 LMG number 841207," I yell. We had been taught to remember the description and serial number of our weapon.

After getting our weapon and two boxes of ammunition, we sprint down the path to our office. According to the evacuation plan, we cannot take any personal items with us—only records—so stopping at the barracks is out of the question. Not that I want to anyway; I just want to get out of here.

I hear the pounding of footsteps all over the compound. There is not much conversation, only a muttered sound or two. The only other sound is noise from the engines of trucks as they line the street, preparing for evacuation.

Truck lights illuminate the brisk night air. Our assigned truck is parked in front of our office, waiting for us to load up.

Burton has already opened the office and moved our locked footlockers toward the door. One locker contains the company finance records, another the personnel records and the last Burton's supervisory files.

"Let's get these on the truck," Burton says. "Then come back and get your backpacks. Then go help Lancaster with the colonel's files."

"Should we load this gun?" I ask, gesturing to the weapon in my hands.

"No. We're not loading shit until we're on the way out of here. When we're out of the compound, then you can do it."

Within a few minutes, all the trucks are loaded.

I hear Captain Hall yelling down the line, "Is everybody ready?"

Our truck is the third in line. Lancaster, Harris and I are sitting in the back with our records.

Burton, who is standing outside our truck, yells, "Ready!" in unison with the others.

I can see the headlights of about 20 other trucks lined up behind us.

"Move out!" comes the command from Captain Hall.

"Yeah, let's get out of here," Harris murmurs.

The trucks start to move forward, but the lead truck stops as we reach the front gate.

An announcement comes over the loudspeaker: "This has been an evacuation drill. Return your weapons to the Arms Room, unload your vehicles and fall into formation at 0500 hours [5 a.m.] in front of the company commander's office."

Curses and outrage can be heard from disgruntled GIs in the trucks all the way down the line.

"Goddamn it, Lancaster! I'm going to kick your ass if you knew about this and didn't tell us," I say.

"I didn't know. I swear," he says as we climb out of the truck. By the way he is shaking, he is probably telling the truth. He's just as scared as the rest of us.

DAYLIGHT IS SLOWLY coming into view as we fall into formation in the street in front of Captain Hall's office. As flag bearer, I'm standing in front of the formation with the American flag.

Captain Hall calls us to attention and says, "Lieutenant Colonel Richmond is now going to address the group."

Richmond steps forward, almost directly in front of me.

I think, "How ridiculous this little man looks in camouflaged fatigues and a combat pack on his back. Burton is much more impressive visually as a leader."

Richmond begins. "Congratulations, men, on the execution this morning of our evacuation plan. It was a total of 49 minutes from the time the alarm sounded until the first truck reached the front gate. Our goal was to accomplish this task in less than an hour, and we succeeded without anyone being hurt or firearms being discharged. Also, for your information, our plan called for two trucks to be dispatched to the line to pick up our guys in the guard posts. The trucks were sent, but we did not actually pull the men off the line. I just wanted you to know that we wouldn't run off and leave them."

There is roaring laughter from the group, which somewhat eases the tension.

"This was a necessary exercise in order for our unit to be prepared to evacuate in a moment's notice. Obviously, the worst time for an evacuation will be while almost everyone is asleep, so that's why we conducted this drill during the middle of the night. Sorry to have interrupted your sleep. Get some rest and enjoy your weekend."

With that, Captain Hall dismisses the company.

After getting the shit scared out of me, I am even more determined to leave the compound as soon as possible.

BUDDY'S LOVE

T IS JULY 16, 1964. As I sip a cup of coffee, which I brought with me from the mess hall after breakfast, I stare at the name "Buddy Davis" on my desk calendar. I have an appointment with him today at the Personnel Office to prepare his pay and personnel records for his rotation back to the States.

I think, "Who in the world would name their child Buddy? Buddy is a nickname, not a real person's name. You name your dog Buddy. You call your best friend Buddy."

Out of curiosity, I thumb through his personnel file to see where he is from.

"That figures," I blurt out to no one in particular.

"What?" Harris asks.

"This guy Davis. He's from Arkansas. A place called Plains."

"He's a hick," Harris says in disgust. "I could have told you that. Anybody who wants to marry one of these Korean whores has got to be from the sticks. How long does he think he's going to be able to keep her down on the farm once he gets her back home?"

"He doesn't need to worry about that," I answer. "I hear that the army denied his request to marry Gina, and you know that his request to extend his tour has been denied. He's on his way out of here."

This is one of the few days when Sergeant Burton is in the office. He chimes in with the fact that the army does an extensive investigation of these brides-to-be before the marriages are sanctioned.

"Character has a lot to do with it. If she's a registered prostitute, the bitch can forget about it," Burton says, showing his disdain for Korean women.

A FEW MINUTES LATER, Buddy comes through the office door. At about 5 feet 11 inches tall, I can picture his thin body as a mechanic in dirty, greasy overalls, working in somebody's auto repair shop alongside the main highway in Plains, Arkansas.

He comes straight to my desk without acknowledging the presence of Burton or Harris. From his demeanor, it is clear that he is not happy with the thought of going home. This is not the same jovial guy I saw a few weeks ago in the restaurant. I sense that this is not the time to engage in friendly, happy conversation that I normally hold with guys who are about to go home. He wants to get this over with and get out of here.

"This is your voucher for travel pay," I say as I hand him the document. "Once you get to the airport tomorrow, the processing center will give you American currency in exchange for the voucher."

Buddy nods.

"How much leave do you plan to take before you report to Fort Riley?"

He is being reassigned to Fort Riley, Kansas, and I think about how lucky he is since Fort Riley is fairly close to his home state of Arkansas.

"None."

"You're not taking any leave?" I ask, startled by his response.

"No," he says without explanation.

"Okay then. See Harris, and he'll go over your reassignment orders. Good luck at your new assignment."

Buddy doesn't say anything. He gets up from the chair at my desk and goes over to see Harris. After a brief conversation with Harris, he is out the door and gone without saying goodbye.

"Weird," Harris says.

I OPEN THE LIBRARY after dinner in the mess hall. I am alone as I begin to shelve several books and magazines that had been left on the tables from the night before.

At about 6:30 p.m., Buddy bursts through the door. I thought I had seen the last of him.

In a panic, he blurts out, "Chris, I need to borrow $10. I'll send it back to you when I get to Fort Riley."

Buddy's eyes are wide open. He is sweating and, from his body language, he is nervous and anxious.

In Korea, GIs are issued military script for currency, and the script has to be turned in prior to departure. Departing GIs are reimbursed in US dollars at the airport for their turned-in script.

"Why do you need money?" I ask. "You're leaving tomorrow. The only place you need money on the compound is at the NCO Club, and I'm sure somebody at the club will buy you a drink."

"I'm going to see if I can sneak into town to see Gina."

Incredibly, this poor sucker was about to marry someone he was still paying for her services. That's why he needs the $10.

"Man, you can't get off this compound. You know that you're restricted to the compound for two weeks prior to rotating back to the States."

"I've got to try. I can't leave without seeing her. Please, man. Let me have the money," he says in desperation.

I reach in my wallet and give him $10. I figure that he has no chance of leaving the compound, but I don't want to argue with him. "Goddamn it. I want my money back today if you don't make it."

"Okay," he says as he snatches the $10 script from my hand and bolts out the door.

WITHIN THE NEXT few hours, Buddy makes several attempts to leave the compound.

First, he goes to the D/O for that day—Sergeant Liggins—and tries to talk his way into a pass to leave the compound. The D/O is provided a list of names each day of those individuals who are restricted to the compound for disciplinary or other reasons. Buddy's name is on the list.

The incident reports, which were ultimately prepared by Specialist Mayfield and Sergeant Liggins and to which I have access, describe the events leading up to Buddy's plight.

After Buddy leaves the Personnel Office, Liggins calls the front gate.

"Specialist Mayfield," says the MP answering the telephone at the front gate.

"This is Sergeant Liggins. Private First Class Buddy Davis is trying to leave the compound. He's scheduled to leave for the States tomorrow. Check all outgoing vehicles to make sure that he's not on one."

"Will do," Mayfield responds.

The hourly bus, which brings workers and GIs back and forth from the south, stops outside the front gate for boarding and unloading. Thus, MPs on duty must check everyone who is coming and going through the gate. The only time the bus ever comes onto the compound is to bring the girls up to the door of the NCO Club for the Saturday night dances.

At 9:00 p.m., Buddy attempts to walk out of the gate to the bus with some of the houseboys who are going off duty.

Mayfield stops him. "Where the f*** do you think you're going? Let me see your pass." He knows that Buddy does not have one.

"Damn. I forgot to get one from the D/O," Buddy says as he turns to walk back into the compound. "I'll be back."

The phone rings on the desk of the D/O.

"Sergeant Liggins."

"Yeah, this is Mayfield at the front gate. That idiot Davis tried to walk out with some of the houseboys. We stopped him. Thought you should know."

"Thanks," Liggins replies.

The lights go out at 10:00 p.m., followed by the customary playing of "Taps" over the company loudspeaker. I lie in my bunk on top of the sheet in my shorts and T-shirt. It is a hot night—July 2—and it is tough trying to fall asleep. The windows of the hooch are open but provide little relief in the way of a breeze. Harris and Lancaster are carrying on some silly chatter in the dark.

BEING THE SENIOR PERSON in the headquarters' hooch, made up of clerical personnel, I had moved into the empty room that should have been occupied by Sergeant Burton, but he had elected to stay alone in a sergeant's hooch.

A few weeks before, Captain Hall conducted a surprise inspection of our hooch. He found the boys engaged in a dice game back in my room and a bottle of scotch whiskey in my nightstand. Gambling and alcohol are prohibited in military barracks.

When Captain Hall entered our hooch to conduct his inspection, I just happened to be leaving the room to go to the latrine.

I yelled, "Attention!"

This order is customary when one first comes into the presence of an officer.

"Carry on," Hall said as I hurried out the door.

I hoped the boys in the back room heard me when I yelled out "Attention!" and were able to stop what they were doing before Hall made it back there.

They didn't make it. One of them was only able to stick the bottle in my nightstand before Hall reached the rear of the hooch.

After leaving the latrine, I didn't return to the hooch. Soon, I heard my name over the loudspeaker with instructions to report to Captain Hall's office.

When I walked into his office, the bottle of whiskey had been placed in the middle of his desk. I pleaded my case by telling him that I don't drink scotch and that the bottle was not mine.

"When you passed me in the doorway," I explained, "I think you would have smelled the alcohol on me if I'd been drinking."

I never drink scotch whiskey. I hate the taste of it.

"It was in your nightstand. It's yours as far as I'm concerned. Anyway, who told you that you could move into the sergeant's room? I want you back in the main bay area of the hooch by tomorrow. Meanwhile, you're restricted to the compound. I'll decide the full extent of your punishment in a few days."

I TWIST IN MY BUNK, trying to fall asleep as I think about my plight and the fact that I brought this upon myself by allowing these young boys to engage in drinking and gambling in my room. After all, I am the ranking person in the hooch and should have asserted some leadership.

A COMPANY COMMANDER has the power to mete out punishment for minor infractions of company rules under Article 15 of the Uniform Code of Military Justice. More serious offenses are subject to a court-martial.

My Article 15 reads, "On or about 2 July 64 at the headquarters barracks, you had in your nightstand one (1) bottle of scotch whiskey. (Article 134) disorder and neglects to the prejudice of good order and discipline in the armed forces."

My punishment: "Restricted to compound #105 for 14 days."

A few days later in his office, Captain Hall confirms this and shows his disappointment after handing me the Article 15. My friendly relationship with him and as his tennis partner come to an end.

I wonder, "Would Hall dare conduct such an inspection of Sergeant Burton's hooch? How many whiskey bottles would he find?"

I DON'T KNOW how long I have been asleep. Someone is running through the dark hooch, knocking over objects. I open my eyes to see the silhouetted bodies of three or four people frantically moving through the room.

"Damn," I think as I cover my head with the sheet. "The North Koreans have invaded us and caught us lying here on our asses."

I am scared shitless. My heart is pounding. Why hasn't the siren sounded to signal that we are being invaded? I wait to be stabbed to death with a bayonet or gunned down in our bunks by machine-gun fire.

Suddenly, the people are gone.

Someone yells out, "What the hell was that?"

I swing my legs out of the bunk. They are shaking so much that I can barely stand up. I cautiously walk to the back door with a few other guys, fully expecting to see North Korean soldiers swarming all over the compound.

Instead, we hear voices of some of our guys yelling to each other about "which way he went." The MPs are chasing someone who is running in and out of the hooches in an attempt to get away.

Lights and noise from a helicopter, which was summoned from the 8th Army hospital in Seoul and is landing at the heliport at the front gate, permeates the hot night air.

I look at my watch: 11:45 p.m.

The MPs finally catch up with and handcuff the person they are chasing: Buddy Davis. I wonder how long he had been running and assume that he gave up from shear exhaustion.

Buddy had viciously stabbed Sergeant Liggins in his right thigh with a 4-inch Bowie knife while scuffling with him when he attempted to try and take a pass from the D/O's desk.

Liggins has already lost a great deal of blood and is in danger of losing his leg. Someone has applied a tourniquet to the leg to stop the bleeding prior to the arrival of the emergency medical personnel. He is evacuated to the hospital immediately.

Buddy is loaded into a truck accompanied by a dozen MPs. He is headed to jail down south with my $10 in his pocket.

He gets his wish. He will not be leaving Korea anytime soon.

BUDDY'S FAITH

AUGUST 25, 1964, is just another long, hot summer day where the heat in Korea is unbearable. I sit at a table in the mess hall, eating dinner with my friend John Gibson. We had both been drafted into the army a year earlier and are congratulating each other on making it to our one-year anniversary.

Dinner consists of roast beef, mashed potatoes and peas. It seems like the army serves roast beef every day, and I am beginning to develop a distinct dislike for the stuff.

I am hoping that John does not bring up the pact that we made at Fort Gordon, Georgia. However, I believe that he knows that I have already broken it. Maybe he has seen me in the village with Mi Chung or maybe he has heard something about us.

I know that John has been true to his wife because he rarely leaves the compound. Instead, he spends most of his free time in the library or at the arts-and-crafts workshop, learning how to develop film in the darkroom and other things. Also, early in his tour, John's peer MPs teased him about his celibacy, but many of them eventually grew to admire and respect his commitment to marriage. Their teasing stopped after a while when his sincerity became apparent.

"You heard from your wife lately?" he asks diplomatically, maybe trying to make me feel guilty.

"She writes about once a week," I answer. "She's doing fine. She's going to graduate from UCLA in a few months. How's your wife?" I ask, quickly trying to divert the conversation.

"Great," he says. "I miss her so much. I can't wait to get out of here."

"Keep the faith. You're doing fine," I say in admiration. "We're past the half-way point of our tour. We'll be home in four months."

AT ABOUT 5:45 P.M., Sergeant Liggins, Specialist Mayfield and two other GIs walk through the mess hall door in their Class-A uniforms. Liggins walks with a limp and cane, but the doctors have managed to save his right leg. It seems as if keeping one's leg is a major problem in the DMZ. Stephen Fisher had not been so lucky.

Sergeant Liggins and his group made it back to the compound in time for dinner after having testified at the court-martial of Buddy Davis in Seoul. Liggins and Mayfield had appeared as witnesses for the prosecution; the two other GIs, one of whom was his motor-pool supervisor Sergeant Graves, were character witnesses.

The men go through the chow line, get their food and sit at a table in the center of the room. Almost everyone gets up and quickly surrounds the men to find out the outcome of Buddy's trial. Liggins sits silently as the others speak. He will be going home now that Buddy's trial is over.

I wonder, "Will Liggins have second thoughts about how he handled the situation with Buddy that night? Did we all underestimate the emotional and psychological trauma that Buddy was going through at the thought of being torn away from Gina? Is the army at fault for not providing Buddy counseling after denying his request for marriage? Maybe someone like Sergeant Graves did counsel him to no avail. Did these things come out at trial?"

I am glad that the question of where Buddy got the money didn't come out at trial. If it had, I may have been blamed in part for his ill-fated attempt to leave the compound that night.

"He got 10 years and was dishonorably discharged from the service," Sergeant Graves says solemnly. "The poor bastard ruined his life.

He'll be spending the next 10 years in federal prison at Fort Leavenworth, Kansas."

It is ironic that Buddy will end up in Kansas anyway but under an entirely different set of circumstances and for a much longer period of time. Maybe Buddy's life, as he saw it, was over anyway without his darling Gina. His one, last, desperate attempt to see her, I think, is testament to the depth of his love for her.

I think about Buddy and John Gibson as I leave the mess hall and walk alone down the path to the library. Both men are making tremendous sacrifices in the name of love. I certainly hope that John's reward will turn out differently than Buddy's.

I'M MR. LONELY

BY SEPTEMBER 1964, Mi Chung has stayed longer with her sick aunt than she had intended. Occasionally, she goes home to see her folks but always returns. We make one attempt to meet in Seoul to do some sightseeing, but the weekend we choose is a bad one because some South Korean workers are engaged in ugly, violent demonstrations over some cause. So, travel by US military is prohibited at that time.

Our dating consists of going to the restaurant and the movie and eventually romance. Perhaps it is a mistake to get too close to Mi Chung. Maybe I am fooling myself to think that our relationship will be nothing more than friendship. Maybe it is something that I desired all along out of loneliness.

Maybe it is too much to ask of young men, who are thrust into a stressful situation such as ours, not to succumb to loneliness and the need for female companionship. After all, many of us have just become sexually active these few years after high school. So, the idea of trying to maintain celibacy for immature young men such as myself is probably a stretch. Many people deal with life's stresses differently. Some use drugs and alcohol, and some have great will power. My way of dealing with stress is with sex.

I do not spend a lot of time with Mi Chung mainly because of the tight space she lives in and because of the language barrier that prevents us from carrying on lengthy, meaningful conversations. Sometimes I bring her old American magazines from the library, which she thoroughly enjoys. I try to bring her black magazines, such as *Ebony*, to show her black people with positive lifestyles and offset some of the negative stereotypes about blacks instilled by some of the Caucasian GIs among Koreans. Also, I try to encourage her to come to the JSA on the bus on Saturday nights, but she refuses. She doesn't want to be associated with the prostitutes.

BURTON'S ARREST

IT IS UNUSUAL for Sergeant Burton not to show up for work on a Monday morning. After all, this is the third Monday in the month, and it is getting close to the time when our payroll must be submitted to the paymaster. His normal routine is to come into the office, review our upcoming week's activities and, once satisfied, disappear back to his hooch to drink.

"You heard from Burton?" I ask Harris.

"No."

"You see him in the mess hall this morning?"

Again, he says, "No."

"Maybe one of us should check on him to see if he's okay."

"I'll check on the drunken bastard as soon as I finish this," Harris says as he bangs away on his typewriter.

On weekends, Sergeant Burton rarely leaves the compound. However, when he does, he goes to Seoul and meets some of his old officer friends who have maintained their friendship despite his fall from grace as an officer.

On one weekend, I ran into him in Seoul at the USO headquarters. He was engaged in friendly chatter with some of the American women who worked in the USO office. On several occasions, I saw some of them chauffeured to our compound to attend parties at our Officers'

Club. I wondered if they knew that Burton was no longer an officer since he was dressed in civilian clothes.

My contact with these USO ladies is connected with our compound library. Being responsible for the library, they occasionally deliver new books to me and assist with the numbering and shelving of the new material. After being away from the States for a while, it is a pleasure to be in the company of American women in Korea even if it is only for a few minutes.

THE TELEPHONE RINGS on my desk.

"The first sergeant wants to see you," says Orlando Dennis, the company clerk. "Can you come to our office now?"

"I'll be right up."

"Barry, First Sergeant Miller wants to see me. I'll be back in a minute."

I head out the door, wondering what he wants and why I have to come to his office. If he wants me to play tennis with him, he normally calls and says to meet him at the tennis court at 4 p.m. I try whenever I can to avoid playing with him because he cheats, often calling balls in or out to his advantage. Outranking me, I can't complain. In spite of our differences on the tennis court, however, I like him. I will forever be grateful to him for pulling me out of the ranks of the MPs and making me the company's finance clerk.

Orlando is sitting behind his desk when I enter the company commander's office. He is a young, black, chubby kid who will occasionally party with us in the village clubs, but no one ever sees him leave with a girl. Some guys speculate that he is a virgin, but I have my doubts. He seems to spend a lot of time horsing around with Lancaster in our hooch, which leads me to believe that they may be of the same persuasion. I have no proof as they manage to keep it in the closet.

"Go on in. He's expecting you," Orlando says, pointing to Miller's office to the left.

Captain Hall's office is to the right. I never want to go into his office again after my encounter with him about the "liquor bottle in my nightstand" incident a few weeks ago.

As I enter Miller's office, he says, "How's everything going this morning in the Personnel Office?"

"Fine. No problems," I say, wondering if I should tell him that Sergeant Burton did not show up this morning.

"Good. You're doing a great job as our finance clerk. I've never had any complaints from our guys regarding their pay since you took over."

"Thanks, Sergeant. I'm glad that you're happy with my performance. You know, I'm forever grateful to you for rescuing me from the DMZ. That is why I let you win a tennis match every now and then," I laugh.

"What? I wish it wasn't so cold. I would take you to the court right now and whip your butt," he shoots back with a grin. "Chris, I need you to be in charge of the Personnel Office for a few days. I know you pretty much run that office anyway."

"Why, may I ask? Did something happen?"

"Sergeant Burton was arrested for assaulting a Korean girl in some village bar over the weekend. He's going to be locked up in jail for a few days."

"I'm shocked," I say in disbelief. "I have never known him to go into any of the local clubs, and I certainly don't believe that he would be messing around with any of the prostitutes."

"I don't have any details, but he will be returning to the compound in a few days. Meanwhile, you're in charge. Come to me if you have any problems that you can't handle."

BACK IN THE OFFICE, I tell Harris about Burton's arrest. We both speculate about how and why Burton was in the village. We surmise that alcohol and his scorn for Korean women have something to do with it.

"One of the barmaids must have come on to him a little too strong and he lost it," I speculate.

I can imagine the misery that Burton must be going through, particularly when it comes to women. Here is a man who at one time was a promotion away from becoming a general. I can see him as a dashing, young, tall and handsome up-and-coming officer who was popular with the ladies. Any man who could entice a general's wife into adultery must have been charming, debonair and persuasive. I picture him dressed in formal military attire at a gala in Washington, DC, or in Europe, dazzling his fellow officers' wives in dinner conversation and while dancing.

I ask myself, "Was he thinking about these things as he attempted to drown his sorrow in alcohol while being pestered by a Korean barmaid to buy her a drink or have sex with her? Did the thought of finding himself in some little, dirty Korean bar—sitting across the table from a Korean whore instead of in an Officers' Club with American female companionship—cause him to unleash his wrath on some poor, unsuspecting girl?"

I can only imagine the demons that he must have been trying to exorcise from his mind when the girl said the wrong thing.

After a few days, Sergeant Burton is returned to the JSA but is restricted to the compound until his pending court-martial in a month. South Korean businesses are heavily dependent on the US military for their economic well-being. Therefore, assaults on Korean nationals by American GIs are tolerated by local authorities who choose not to prosecute under local law for fear of losing military business. Instead, they leave resolution of such issues to the US military justice system.

BURTON'S TRIAL

FOR A MONTH, Sergeant Burton says little or nothing about the incident involving his alleged assault on the Korean barmaid. The subject only comes up when he leaves the office to go down to 8th Army headquarters in Seoul to meet with his court-appointed attorney.

One morning, while sitting at his desk, he mutters something about "that damn Korean bitch causing me all this trouble" while researching the Uniform Code of Military Justice.

Burton had been tried once by a court-martial and then booted out of the military, so it is obvious that he is quite concerned this time—so concerned that he has stopped drinking and has been sober for the past several weeks. His hands no longer shake in the morning while trying to drink a cup of coffee. He may have been advised by his attorney to stop drinking prior to his trial, or he may have stopped on his own due to the seriousness of the matter.

IT IS THE MORNING of November 20. Sergeant Burton stops by the office prior to leaving for his court-martial in Seoul.

I see a side of him that I have not seen before: distinguished military officer. The transformation is amazing. His demeanor has changed. I can see that, at one time, this man had class. His appearance has changed. He is clean-shaven, and his hair is well groomed. He looks neater in his uniform than I have ever seen him. His black shoes are spotless. The display of ribbons and citations on the left side of his chest is impressive, including a Distinguish Service Cross, a Valorous Unit Award, a Purple Heart Medal, a Silver Star Medal, a Parachutist Badge, a World War II Victory Medal and a Combat Action Ribbon. He may have been stripped of his officer rank, but nobody can take away his many awards and citations.

Burton walks and talks like a person of distinction. He easily out-classes every officer on the compound including Lieutenant Colonel Richmond.

At about 9 a.m., Harris and I wish Burton well as he leaves the office. Captain Hall has to accompany Burton to court but refuses to ride in the same vehicle with him, choosing instead to drive his private jeep with another officer. Burton rides in a jeep behind them, accompanied by two MPs. Harris and I watch the caravan leave the compound.

"You think we will ever see him again?" Harris asks. "If he is convicted and has to do time, will they let him come back and pack up his things, or will he go straight to jail?"

"I don't know. Maybe we should have asked him. Hell, how do you talk to somebody about a thing like that?" I wonder aloud.

I like Sergeant Burton as a boss because he stays out of our way and pretty much lets me run the Personnel Office. Also, he went to bat for me when Captain Hall wanted to take away my stripe for 30 days because of the "liquor bottle in my nightstand" incident.

During a ride to pick up the payroll, Sergeant Burton told me of a conversation he had with Captain Hall.

"Goddamn it, Junior," Burton had said to Hall. "You're being too hard on my guy. All he had was a bottle of whiskey in his nightstand, and he doesn't even drink the stuff. It's obvious that someone else put it there. He's a married man and needs his money. Confine him to the compound for a few weeks. That's punishment enough."

"Stop calling me Junior," Hall had responded. "I demand that you respect me as your commanding officer, even when we're riding alone."

Superior military officers frequently refer to lower-ranked officers as "junior officers," so that was Burton's way of letting Hall know that he once was superior in rank to him. "Junior" became the secret nickname that Burton, Harris and I called Captain Hall anytime we talked about him.

"I'll think about it," Hall told Burton in reference to the punishment.

During these payroll runs to Seoul, Burton told me that Captain Hall would often ask questions about matters that would help enhance his career. Hall knew that Burton had climbed the military ladder to the rank of full-bird colonel and would also know something about what it would take to get to the top. Also, Hall understood that Burton may still know people in important places who could torpedo his career, so he tolerated his disrespectfulness when they were alone. To Burton's credit, he was always respectful to Hall in the presence of other people, calling him "Sir" and saluting him when appropriate. That's when I saw that Burton had a serious commitment to the military and to its protocol.

THE DAY DRAGS ON. Harris and I do our mundane office work, trying not to think too much about the plight of Sergeant Burton. However, the subject inevitably comes up.

"I hope he gets off," Harris says, breaking the silence in the office.

I light a cigarette and lean back in my chair, thinking about what Harris just said.

"You know, as much as I like Burton, I dislike the idea of a man hitting a woman—any woman—even if she is a Korean whore. She's just another human being, trying to scratch out a living in this country under some miserable circumstances. We're supposed to be here to protect these people, not bring further grief upon them. If he's guilty, then he should pay the price for his actions. It's not her fault that the son of a bitch screwed up his life."

"You think that was behind it?" Harris asks me. "He was feeling sorry for himself and took it out on the Korean girl?"

"Why do you think he drinks so much?" I wonder aloud. "He's trying to drown his past in alcohol. I'm sure he hears the laughter and fun coming from the Officers' Club. The thought of someone like Captain Hall and other junior officers partying with the American females from down south or with the foreign women from the Swiss/Swede camp must drive him crazy, knowing that he should be there too. Instead, he is relegated to a sleazy Korean bar with some young girl rubbing up against him and asking, 'GI, you want have good time?'"

IT IS ABOUT 4:00 P.M. when Harris notices Captain Hall's familiar green-and-white jeep flash by the window, heading up the road toward his office.

"Junior is back. He just went by."

"Is the other jeep behind him, Barry?"

"No."

"Shit. It must not have gone so well."

THE EVENING IS turning dark. After about an hour, headlights from a second jeep shine outside our window as it stops to let Burton out. He doesn't come into our office but instead heads up the path to his quarters.

"There he is. Let's find out what happened," Harris says.

"Give him a minute," I suggest. "He may want to be alone. It may be why he didn't come in here."

Unable to wait any longer, we close the office a few minutes before our customary time of 5:30 p.m. Lancaster hasn't been here, so we guess that he doesn't know either. We hurry up the path to Burton's hooch and tap on the door, asking if we can come in.

"Come on in, you crazy bastards," Burton says in a laughing and jovial manner. He is probably on his second or third drink.

As I enter the hooch, Burton slaps me on the shoulder and hugs me tightly, and then he does the same thing to Harris. I can tell from his hug that he is sincere, as if we are his family and he wants to share some good news with us.

He still has on his uniform, but his shirt is open down the front and pulled out from around his waist. His dog tags dangle around his neck outside his white undershirt. His shoes are off, but he still has on his socks as he walks around the hooch, trying to find two cups in which to pour us a drink. It is obvious that he is in a celebratory mode, so trying to beg off drinking with him is out of the question. He drinks straight bourbon whiskey with no ice or chaser. I accept my cup but don't drink what's in it. I am anxious to hear what happened.

Burton finally sits on his bunk and starts to talk. Harris sits on the unoccupied bunk across from Burton. Although several new sergeants have come to the unit, no one is willing to share a hooch with him. I pull up a chair and sit between the two men.

AS BURTON DESCRIBES IT, the courtroom is typically military. The clerk of the court reads the charges against him and the proceedings begin. The first and only witness that the presiding officer Captain Joseph Pierce can come up with is the victim herself: Kim Han. The bar owner and other Korean nationals, who may have witnessed the incident, have refused to testify for fear of retaliation against their establishment by the US military.

A male Korean interpreter accompanies Kim Han to the witness stand and asks, "Do you swear to tell the truth, nothing but the truth, so help you God?"

The interpreter repeats the question in Korean.

"I do," Ms. Han answers in Korean as she nervously takes the witness chair.

"You may now question the witness," the presiding judge bellows.

At this point, Burton leans over to his court-appointed attorney and whispers, "Ask her if she believes in God as she attested when she was sworn in."

"Ms Han. You just swore to tell the truth on a bible. Do you believe in God?"

The interpreter restates the question in Korean.

"Buddha. I believe in Buddha," she responds in Korean.

Burton leans over and confers with his attorney before the next question. It is apparent that he is calling the shots.

The attorney addresses the court. "Your honor, I submit to you that this witness is not eligible to testify in a US military court proceeding because she has lied under oath. She swore before God that she would tell the truth. In fact, she does not believe in God. She believes in Buddha."

"Objection!" the presiding officer yells as he jumps to his feet. "May we approach the bench?"

The presiding judge summons both attorneys to the bench. After a much-heated discussion, he orders both attorneys to step back.

"My ruling is that this witness cannot testify in these proceedings unless she will swear before God to the truthfulness of her testimony according the Uniform Code of Military Justice." Then the judge turns and asks the interpreter, "Will she do that?"

The interpreter restates the judge's question.

Ms. Han responds in Korean and says, "Buddha."

Burton's attorney reiterates, "She only believes in Buddha, your honor."

"Then I declare this witness ineligible to testify in this court. Please tell Ms. Han thank you and that she is free to go. Do you have any other witnesses, Captain Pierce?"

"No, your honor."

"Okay then. It is the ruling of this court that there is insufficient evidence to substantiate the charges against the defendant. Therefore, all charges are dismissed. Sergeant Burton, you're free to go. Please see the clerk of the court for your dismissal papers."

"Thank you, your honor," Burton says as he stands up and shakes his attorney's hand, holding back his jubilation. He knows that he has just dodged a bullet, so he is not about to offend the court.

Captain Hall comes up to Burton and shakes his hand, saying that he hopes he has learned his lesson from this experience and that he should stay out of Korean nightclubs if he can't control his temper.

"I'll see you back at the compound," Hall says as he walks away.

Burton remains behind to obtain his dismissal papers.

BURTON REACHES OVER to his nightstand, grabs the bottle of whiskey and pours himself another drink as he marvels in delight at his courtroom brilliance. The bastard never mentions whether or not he was guilty as charged.

"Now that this episode is over," I say, "I just want to know what in the hell were you doing in that Korean bar in the first place? I've never known you to frequent any of the local clubs in the area."

"I was coming back from Seoul, and I needed a drink. I got off the bus in that village because I couldn't wait until I got back to the compound."

I have never been this close to anyone who is so addicted to alcohol. This man has a serious problem, and he is going right back to what got him into trouble in the first place. Sooner or later, drinking is going to lead to his demise if he doesn't get help. Maybe Captain Hall will insist that he seek counseling, but I doubt it. He would just as soon be rid of Burton one way or another.

"Damn," I think as I get up to leave. "Come on, Barry. Let's go to dinner. See you later, Sarg."

AS I AM LEAVING the Personnel Office with Harris on the afternoon of November 25—a few days after Burton's court-martial—Sergeant Burton asks me to stop by his hooch sometime the next day because he wants to talk to me. The next day is Thanksgiving, so the office will be closed.

"Sure. I'll stop by before I go to dinner."

I have no idea what Burton wants to talk about, but it is apparently something that he does not want to discuss in the presence of Harris.

The next day, I go to Burton's hooch at about 2:30 p.m., fully expecting to find him half-tanked. Surprisingly, he is sober, neatly dressed and well groomed. I sit on the still unoccupied bunk opposite his.

"Sit down, Chris. I'll get right to the point. You'll probably be leaving soon from all indications, so I want to talk to you privately before then. During the time I've worked with you, I have been impressed with your intelligence, maturity and ability to communicate. You handle yourself well and display outstanding leadership qualities. You are a good role model for Harris and some of the other young fellows in your hooch. They listen to you, and you have kept them on the straight and narrow, for the most part, except for that liquor-bottle incident a few months ago."

"Thanks for the compliment, Sarg. As you know, I just turned 25 a few days ago, so I'm rather old compared to these 18- and 19-year-old kids. It's the price I have to pay for being drafted at 23."

"Yes," Burton continues, "but I also observe that you handle yourself well with older servicemen and officers while dealing with their pay matters. In short, I think you are officer material and should consider re-enlisting and going to Officer Candidate School after this tour of duty is completed. I still have some contacts in Washington who will gladly recommend you for OCS based upon my recommendation. The army needs a whole lot more black officers now that the services have been integrated. It's wide open for you."

"Man, I don't know. I have never thought about staying in the army. You're right though. I encountered only one black first lieutenant at Fort Leonard Wood and one black captain at Fort Gordon since I've been in the service. It's interesting that you would recommend the army as a career choice after the way you've been treated."

"The army has been good to me," Burton shares. "I had a very good career before my self-destructive behavior did me in. It wasn't the army's fault. Alcohol and women were my downfall. Stay away from those things, and you'll be alright. I know about your little fling in the village. You're married, so you're going to have to learn to be true to your vows; otherwise, that type of behavior will get you into a lot of trouble. Take it from someone who knows," he adds, looking down in deep reflection.

This is the first time I have ever heard Burton even hint at his sins of the past. I am flattered that he would confide in me. Also, I am moved by his compassion for the army and his desire to improve it by encouraging young, black soldiers to make the army a career choice and to seek higher positions in it.

"You're right," I say. "I'm not happy with myself for yielding to temptation during my stay in Korea. I was raised better than that."

I am not comfortable with this conversation, so I hurriedly return to the purpose of our discussion. "I doubt if a career in the military is for me. I can't see Evelyn being a military wife, moving around from place to place. She will soon finish UCLA and will want to pursue her own career. In addition, I have a big problem not being able to control where I live and raise my family. I can't take the bigotry and racism that I experienced in Missouri and Georgia if I can help it. I've lived in California too long."

"Son," Burton adds, "unfortunately you're going to experience those things no matter where you live, even in California. Things are beginning to change back home. Civil-rights laws are being passed. Attitudes are changing. Race relations are improving in the South. I understand that your wife may not want to move from place to place. My wife has long since decided to stay in Arizona and leave the traveling to me. Early in my career, she enjoyed living abroad and seeing different parts of the world, but the novelty soon wore off as the years went by and she craved more stability."

I don't mention it to Burton, but another reason I will not stay in the army is the conflict in Vietnam, which seems to be escalating into a full-blown war. So far, I have dodged that bullet, and I'm not going to put myself in harm's way again if I survive my last nine months in the army.

As I get up to leave, I thank Sergeant Burton for his kind words and faith in me. I promise him that I will give it some thought and stay in touch in case I need the recommendation he has promised.

In bed, I reflect on our conversation. Undoubtedly, he is the most intriguing person I have encountered thus far in the military. I wish I had the chance to get to know him better. Unfortunately, his days of sobriety are few and far between.

OPERATION SANTA CLAUS

ALTHOUGH I AM NOT scheduled to leave Korea until January 23, 1965, in early December, I learn that I am eligible to go home early because my departure date is within 30 days of Christmas, under what the US Army calls "Operation Santa Claus." The only other criterion is that my replacement has to arrive and be oriented in his duties. Fortunately, my unit does not want to be without a finance clerk again, as was the case when I was found within the ranks, so my replacement has been requisitioned well before my departure, and he has already arrived.

Suddenly, by the second week in December, I am confined to the compound because I am within two weeks of going home. Thus, I never have a chance to go into the village to say goodbye to Mi Chung.

However, on December 21, I am allowed to go with my unit on a bus down to Inchon to see Bob Hope's USO Christmas Show, which was coming through Korea on its way back from Vietnam. This turns out to be one of the most enjoyable experiences I have had in Korea. For many years, Bob Hope has been entertaining American troops abroad during the holidays, so it is a thrill to see him with entertainers like Phyllis Diller, Anita Bryant, Miss World, Les Brown, Joey Heatherton and Vic Damone.

Bob Hope tour

I AM SITTING on my bunk, slowly packing clothes into my duffel bag and preparing for my trip home tomorrow. John Gibson drops in to say goodbye, and we reminisce about our year in Korea, wishing each other well. John had arrived in Korea a few weeks after I did, so his tour of duty will not end until sometime in February and is not eligible to go home early for the holidays under the Operation Santa Claus rule.

"John, there have been many days during the past year when I thought this moment would never come. I've seen a lot, experienced a lot and witnessed a lot. If I wasn't a man when I came here, I think I certainly am now. I think that anybody who can survive under this intense pressure, sitting in isolation at the doorstep of a communist regime for a year, is now ready to face anything in life."

"Yeah, Chris. We've seen some guys who couldn't handle it and didn't make it out of here in one piece. You've done well and distinguished yourself while you were here."

"I've made mistakes and did some things I'm not proud of," I admit. "At times, I succumbed to the pressures of loneliness and fear, and seemingly abandoned my Christian beliefs, but many a night I prayed to God for forgiveness of my sins and asked for strength to persevere. I'm living proof of his forgiveness and that he truly does answer prayers."

"I know you're a good person, Chris. I saw you in church service a few times over the past few months."

At that moment, Harris comes through the door of the hooch and blurts out, "Chris, your old lady is at the club, demanding to see you. She came on the bus."

I am embarrassed that Harris mentions Mi Chung in front of John at a time when I am going through a moment of soul searching.

"What did you tell her?"

"I didn't tell her that you are leaving," Harris says. "I told her that I thought you were working in the library."

"Good. Tell her that I can't come. Anyway, I've turned in my olive greens, so I can't get into the dance anyway."

"She's threatening to come and find you if don't show up," Harris adds. "I think you had better find a way to come to the club."

"Chris, we're about the same size," offers John. "I'll get a pair of my olive greens. I think you'd better go and see her. You don't want any trouble on your last night here."

"Thanks, man," I say, feeling disgusted that I have to stop what I am doing and deal with a problem that I have created.

THE NIGHT IS TURNING extremely cold as I hurry up the path to the NCO Club. I think about how I will have to tell Mi Chung that I am leaving sooner than expected and I am sorry that our friendship has to end so abruptly. She knows that my tour in Korea is due to end sometime early in 1965, but we have never discussed exactly when it was going to happen.

As I enter the NCO Club and show my membership card to the guys at the door, they playfully threaten not to let me in because the name on the card does not match the name tag "Gibson" on my uniform. The NCO Club has a $5 monthly membership fee, and you are issued a membership card each month.

"The John Gibson we know wouldn't come near any of the girls in here," one guy laughs.

"Come on," I say. "I still have time to mess up your pay before I leave."

"Oh, then by all means, come on in, Mr. Washington!"

The club is alive with dancing and loud music as I walk in, trying to acclimate my vision to the dimly lit room. Before I can locate Mi Chung and Harris, a few well-wishers pull me over to the bar, which is located immediately to the left of the door, to buy me a farewell drink. I am not the only one leaving, so there are several celebrations going on. Five of us will be on our way home tomorrow.

One of the men in the group is Specialist James Allen, who is one of two MPs accompanying the girls to our club from their pickup spot at the front gate of Camp Casey. One MP sits in the back of the bus and the other sits up front to handle any confrontations that might take place among the girls.

I ask Allen, "How did Mi Chung get on the bus?"

"As the last girl came on the bus and the driver closed the door," Allen explains, "another girl came out of nowhere and softly tapped on the door, asking to come aboard. After the girl stepped onto the bus, she was immediately confronted by Mona.

"Mona yelled at the girl, 'Where the f*** do you think you're going?'

"I told Mona to shut up and told the girl to sit up front with me. Then I recognized that she was your girlfriend Mi Chung."

"Thanks for looking after her, and please watch her when they return to the village tonight," I request.

"I will."

I WALK ACROSS the dance floor, trying to find the booth where Mi Chung is sitting. The Supremes are singing, "Where Did Our Love Go."

Suddenly, Mona grabs my hand, and I find myself dancing with her and three other girls. The drink I had at the bar is beginning to take effect, so I am now in a partying mode. I dance with one girl at a time while the other three encircle us. Another record starts to play, so we dance some more. I am having a good time and briefly forget what brought me to the club in the first place.

Harris finally comes onto the dance floor and pulls me away.

Mona is visibly irritated at Harris for taking me away. She curses at him in Korean as he leaves, ignoring her tirade.

"We're over here," Harris says as he leads me to a booth toward the center of the club. "I'm tired of babysitting your woman."

"I'm sorry, man. Everyone seems to have pounced on me the minute I walked through the door. Go buy you a drink," I say as I hand him a couple of script dollars that I had borrowed from John.

I slide into the seat next to Mi Chung and kiss her on the cheek. A big grin comes across her face as she wraps her arms around me and hugs me tightly. She seems relieved to see me. She has been sitting in the club for an hour or so, virtually alone in an atmosphere totally out of her element. The other girls are drinking, dancing and having a good time while she sits, not knowing what has become of me.

She plays with the straw in her Coke as she bashfully stares at the table. She still has her coat on although the smoke-filled club is quite warm and balmy.

"You finally decided to come to a dance," I say, knowing that it is probably not the purpose of her visit.

"Where you been? I had to come find you."

"I've been busy, Mi Chung. I couldn't come into the village for a few weeks. Let me take off your coat," I say as I reach around her shoulders.

The booth is small, and she motions that she will have to slide out to take off her coat. I get up and hold her hand as she slides out of the seat. She takes off her coat and stands momentarily as if waiting for me to say something. Her beautiful, black, silky hair is shoulder length and shaped like a bell on the top of her head.

"Is it something about the way she looks? Does she want to dance? What is it?" I silently wonder.

She takes my hand and places it on her protruding stomach. "You *papa*."

"What?"

I recognize the word *papa* in Korean. My knees buckle as I fall back into the seat. This is the last thing I expected to hear from her. It had only been three weeks since I last saw her, and there was no indication that she was pregnant.

"How can this be?" I wonder again.

Mi Chung is still standing at the side of the table. I gather my composure and reach out and hug her around the waist after it hits me that she is carrying my child. I rub her stomach to see if I can feel the baby.

"How long?"

"Maybe five months," she says, holding out five fingers.

"How long have you known about the baby?"

She hunches her shoulders as if to say that she doesn't know. The question is probably too tough for her to try and answer in English. Anyway, she must have known for a while but was scared to tell me for fear of losing me.

"Is this why she came up tonight?" I ask myself. "Maybe she thought I was aware of her pregnancy and had abandoned her."

IT IS 11:00 P.M., and the bus will be leaving at midnight to take the girls back to the village. Suddenly, I have less than an hour to tell this girl, who is carrying my baby, that I am leaving and, most likely, she and the child would never see me again.

I decide to tell her that I am leaving but not that it will be at 6:30 a.m. I don't know how she will react to that news here on the compound. I lead her to believe that I will have a chance to see her again in a few days before I leave for home.

"I'll come and see you next week, and then we'll talk about the baby," I say, knowing that such a conversation, to my relief, will never take place. I wouldn't know what to say to her anyway. Being five months pregnant, she probably has already made up her mind that she is going to keep the baby, and I wouldn't discourage her otherwise as the thought of aborting a child is repugnant to me.

She nods in agreement as I put my arm around her and assure her that everything will be all right.

I feel terrible about the baby. Although I didn't ask for this child, the fact that it is mine and that I will be leaving him or her in this dreadful country, relegated to a life of despair and most likely poverty, are more than I can bear. Also, the child could end up being raised in one of the many Korean orphanages for mixed American GI children if Mi Chung chooses not to keep it.

The lights in the club begin to blink, signaling that it is close to midnight and time for the girls to get on the bus. I help Mi Chung put on her coat and walk her to the bar where I buy her a souvenir silver mug with the last $5 in my pocket. The mug is engraved "JSA, Panmunjom Korea" with the UNC Military Armistice Commission's blue-and-white symbol.

"Something for you to drink your tea in," I say as I hand her the box and kiss her on the cheek.

She smiles as she slips the box into her coat pocket and gets in line with the other girls to board the bus. Some of the guys, like me, walk with our girls all the way to the door of the bus to savor the last moment. Also, by this time, a few of the girls—like Mona—are loud, argumentative with each other and highly intoxicated. Some are trying to sing in broken English the last song they heard as they left the club.

Specialist Allen, still on duty at the door of the bus and looking as if he is dreading this final bus ride, tries to hurry the girls out of the cold and onto the bus.

"Looks like you guys are going to have your hands full going back. Watch out for my girl," I tell Allen.

"I will. She sits up front with me."

"You come see me. You promise," Mi Chung says as she hugs me for the last time and steps onto the bus.

"I promise."

DECEMBER 23 AT 6 A.M. is the start of one of the happiest and saddest days of my life. Five of us shiver in the morning cold as we wait in front of the company commander's office for the truck that will transport us to Kimpo International Airport. In addition to our duffel bags, each of us has a 3-foot by 5-foot wooden box, which is provided by the military, to take home other items such as souvenirs. One of the items taking up most of the space in my box is a 10-place setting of bone-china dishes that I bought for my mother.

A canvas-back truck pulls up within minutes, and we load our stuff onto the back. D/O Sergeant Hendricks comes out of the office to check our reassignment orders and clears us to leave the compound.

In parting, he says, "On behalf of the United States Army and the United Nations Command Military Armistice Commission, I want to thank each one of you for your service in Korea and, in particular, for serving your tour of duty in the Joint Security Area inside the DMZ. I wish you well at your new assignment."

The two-hour ride to the airport in the back of the open-ended truck is unpleasant on this cold, 18-degree F winter morning, but nobody complains. The MPs on duty hoop, holler and wave goodbye as the truck pulls out of the front gate. In my 12 months in Korea, I have never witnessed the actual moment of somebody leaving, so the fanfare by the MPs as we depart is a pleasant surprise.

As the truck heads up the road toward the bridge, I look back one final time at the compound and the overhead sign at the gate: "Stop. You're About to Enter the Demilitarized Zone." A wealth of emotions comes over me as I realize that I have survived and most likely will never have to enter the DMZ again. I say "most likely" because I still have another eight months in the army, so conceivably I could find myself back here if war breaks out with North Korea.

Within a few minutes, we are traveling south across the bridge—this beautiful, lumpy bridge; this bridge to freedom. This same bridge was the escape route for thousands of Koreans who were fleeing from the north about 10 years ago. This same bridge was my escape route on the weekends, only to bring me back for another week of agony inside the DMZ.

In 1953, General Douglas MacArthur and his troops crossed this bridge going north, hell bent on chasing the North Koreans all the way to China, and his overzealousness cost him his job. When he came back across this bridge going home, MacArthur would soon be fired by President Harry Truman for disobedience.

My final journey across this bridge will hopefully be more rewarding.

I SIT ON THE BENCH on one side of the truck with a guy named Kenneth Trask, a friend with whom I had attended basic and MP training. The other three men face us on the other side. Our boxes and duffel bags are loaded in the center aisle toward the front of the truck.

During the two-hour ride, we don't say much to each other. Four of us younger guys engage in idle chatter about where we are being reassigned and our leave plans before reporting to our new assignments. Of course, I am quite familiar with each of my travel mates since I had, sometime during the prior two weeks, sat with them to prepare their pay and personnel records for departure.

The fifth guy is an old, grizzled motor-pool sergeant named Jimmy Wardlow. He is unshaven with a gray, stubbly beard several weeks old. His superior officers have probably long since given up talking to him about good grooming. His red, weather-beaten face is wrinkled and his calloused hands are hard and battered, showing many years underneath the hoods of jeeps and trucks all over the world.

As I stare at Wardlow, I wonder silently if he could service a tank. I guess he probably could. He is a career serviceman who has spent a prior tour of duty in Korea. He sits silently and appears to be indifferent to this whole experience of going home after being out of the States for a long time. Most likely, he will come back to Korea before his career is over.

WE LOOK OUT of the back end of the truck as it speeds along the bumpy road on our journey to Kimpo International Airport. Befittingly, it is as if we are leaving the country of Korea behind inch by inch, mile by mile. The truck arrives at Yong Ju Gol and slowly winds its way down the center street of the village.

I look back at the entry gate to Camp Casey, the photography studio on the left where I first met Mi Chung and the alley on the right where I spent so many nights drinking and partying in the black clubs. It is still early morning, so not too many people are on the street.

However, a Korean ambulance, which is parked in front of Black Alley, catches my eye. The alley is too narrow for vehicles. I wonder if the ambulance is for Mi Chung's sickly aunt or for some other old person who lives along the fringes of the village. Also, there is an unoccupied MP jeep parked nearby, so whatever the problem in the alley is, it must have involved an American GI.

Yong Ju Gol slowly fades out of view and, with it, a lot of fond and sad memories. I am leaving a child—my child—in that alley.

"What kind of Christmas will it have a year from now?" I wonder silently.

AS WE TRAVEL along the road, I stare at my fellow passengers and wonder how many children they are leaving behind.

"What about old Wardlow? How many bastard children does he have scattered throughout the world? Maybe none. Maybe I'm judging him unfairly based on his appearance. Maybe he possesses the necessary moral fiber to fight those sexual urges that I find lacking in me."

It makes me sick to my stomach to think that, during my stay here, I have succumbed to a degree of unethical behavior that I will regret for the rest of my life.

IT IS AUGUST 20, 1965, and I am traveling from St. Louis, Missouri, to my home in Los Angeles after being honorably discharged from the army. Incredibly, I had been reassigned to Fort Leonard Wood for my last eight months of service after my one-year stint in Korea. At least I was familiar with the territory and did not have to acclimate to new surroundings and another city.

I land at the airport and, on my ride home, I notice National Guardsmen standing guard on several street corners in my community. Civil unrest in the form of riots has consumed parts of the city, and the guardsmen have been placed there to restore order.

Sergeant Burton was right. Civil unrest can happen anywhere, even in California.

Welcome home.

EPILOGUE

IN THE EARLY 1970S, President Richard Nixon embarked upon a policy to reduce US forces in South Korea by 20,000. Called the Nixon Doctrine, the subsequent troop withdrawal had profound consequences for the many Korean villages that had flourished around military installations. While some villages like Yong Ju Gol disappeared, others expanded and flourished.

In Katharine H.S. Moon's book, *Sex Among Allies: Military Prostitution in U.S.–Korea Relations*, she reports that, in 1971, tensions between the Korean and US governments came to a head after the reduction of US forces. Further, in a campaign to persuade the United States to maintain its military presence, the Korean government initiated a Clean-Up Campaign to stamp out VD and extend control over prostitution, particularly around US bases. Prostitutes were to become, in effect, unofficial ambassadors between the two nations.

Despite four decades of coexistence in the JSA between UNC forces and the North Koreans, the truce between the two sides is still fragile. The potential volatility of this relationship was never more demonstrated when, on August 18, 1976, the UNC and civilian Korean workers attempted to prune a large poplar tree, which was obstructing the view between UNC Posts #3 and #4.

Suddenly, a large contingent of North Korean soldiers appeared and demanded that the pruning be stopped. When Captain Arthur

Bonifas, the D/O in charge, did not order the work stopped, the North Koreans attacked, using pick handles and axes that the group had been using to trim the tree. In the skirmish—later known as the Axe Murder Incident—Captain Bonifas and another officer were hacked to death and several other UNC workers were wounded. The JSA was subsequently renamed Camp Bonifas in memory of one of the two slain officers.

On January 29, 2002, in his State of the Union speech, President George W. Bush referred to North Korea as an "axis of evil" because of the regime's treatment and starvation of its people. Later that year, he visited the DMZ and Camp Bonifas.

Upon hearing of the Axe Murder Incident, Bush told a reporter, "Did you hear that? No wonder I think they're evil."

I NEVER KNEW the fate of Mi Chung until Barry Harris contacted me a few years later when he came to Los Angeles to visit his mother. He had finished his tour of duty in the army but was considering re-enlisting for another four years of service.

While having dinner in a restaurant, I noticed how Barry had grown into manhood and was not the brash, immature, 18-year-old whom I knew in Korea. We both brought pictures from our days while working and playing in Korea. One of my pictures was of Mi Chung and me, taken in the NCO Club the night before I left Korea.

"I hate that I left Korea knowing that Mi Chung was pregnant and that I would probably never see her or our newborn child," I admitted to Barry.

"I wanted to write and tell you what happened the morning you left," Barry said, "but I could not risk putting anything in writing, knowing that you were married. When the girls returned to Yong Ju Gol that night from the dance, Mi Chung was beaten up pretty badly in the alley by Mona and some of her friends as she was trying to go home. I believe they were jealous of the relationship that Mi Chung had with you and the fact that she was not really one of them—you know, one of the working girls. Anyway, unknown to them, Mi Chung

130

had the metal JSA cup you had given her under her coat, which pressed into her stomach during the assault. She lived but unfortunately lost her baby. The girls were subsequently tried and convicted of manslaughter and sent to prison for a few years."

"Goddamn! I told the MPs that night to watch Mi Chung as she got off the bus in the village to see that nothing happened to her. Mona was giving her a bad time when they got onto the bus before leaving the JSA."

"You're lucky that you were able to leave Korea that day. When the local police found the mug on Mi Chung, they assumed that an American GI from the JSA had beat her up. She was unconscious and could not tell them who had assaulted her. The MPs contacted Captain Hall, who then talked to the JSA MPs on duty the night before. They said that the Korean girl had been seen with you at the dance, but they assured him that she was okay when she boarded the bus to take them back to town that night. Captain Hall still wanted to call the airport to stop you from leaving pending further investigation, but Sergeant Burton spoke up for you and insisted that you had nothing to do with what happened in the village and to let you go home to your family."

"I had no idea that was going on," I said. "Man, I owe Sergeant Burton a lot."

REFLECTING ON my year in the DMZ, I realized that this story is not so much about a military unit performing duty on a small strip of land that, for years, has divided the country of Korea and its people. Rather, it tells the story about relationships and how we interact with each other as human beings.

www.ingramcontent.com/pod-product-compliance
Lightning Source LLC
Chambersburg PA
CBHW050950050726
47592CB00007B/2515